ZANE GREY
A Photographic Odyssey

ZANE GREY
A Photographic Odyssey

LOREN GREY

TAYLOR PUBLISHING COMPANY
Dallas, Texas

Published by Taylor Publishing Company
1550 West Mockingbird Lane, Dallas, Texas 75235

Library of Congress Cataloging in Publication Data

Grey, Loren.
  Zane Grey: a photographic odyssey.
    1. Grey, Zane, 1872-1939 — Journeys — Pictorial works.
2. Novelists, American — 20th century — Biography —
Pictorial works. 3. Voyages and travels — Pictorial works.
I. Title.
PS3513. R6545Z64   1985   813'.52   85-4644
ISBN 0-87833-462-9

Printed in the United States of America

First Edition 0 9 8 7 6 5 4 3 2 1

TO CAROL BROWN

*Who, I believe, sees in my father's writing reflections of
his universal love of Nature and of the nobility of the human spirit.
In a very true sense, they seem to be her feelings as well.
Her enthusiasm may well explain why Zane Grey's books will
continue to be read as avidly as hundred years from now as they are today.*

PREFACE

As the photographs in this volume attest, Zane Grey actually lived the rugged and exciting life about which he wrote so vividly. As a boy, he fished and hunted in the Ohio River Valley; when a young man, around the Delaware and Lackawaxen Rivers and on trips to Tampico and Yucatan in Mexico. On his first travels to the West he rode horses for endless hours over blazing deserts and rugged mountain trails, and he roped wild mountain lions in the Grand Canyon with a character named "Buffalo" Jones. Later, when he became successful as a writer, Zane Grey visited the magnificent Rainbow Bridge only four years after its discovery, hunted bear and wild turkey in the Tonto Basin, and ran the treacherous rapids of the Rogue and North Umpqua Rivers in Oregon in search of the elusive steelhead trout. All of these adventures he not only wrote about but documented on film, with many stills and thousands of feet of motion picture film.

Eventually, his travels were to lead to far away places: from Florida and Nova Scotia to Catalina Island, then eventually to the remote reaches of the South Pacific — Tahiti, the mysterious Tuamotu Islands, Tonga and Fiji, and finally, New Zealand and Australia. From these travels came more than two million words of unforgettable prose, fiction and non-fiction, and a wealth of photography. Only a few of the very finest photographs could be reproduced here. However, I feel that this collection — many of these photographs have never before been published — affords a priceless accompaniment to the achievements of one of the most extraordinary outdoorsmen and writers of our time.

Collating and selecting these photographs, though occupying a period of several years, was as much a labor of love as it was labor. As an amateur photographer myself, fortunate enough to have accompanied my father on many of his later expeditions, I was able, not only to appreciate how these photos were taken, but did indeed shoot some of them myself. Of course, it was necessary to eliminate many pictures, but perhaps someday those can be included in a subsequent volume. I feel my selections represent the best of those I considered for presentation. I do gratefully acknowledge the help of Glen Iwasaki in this selection; as an ardent fisherman, I would probably have included many more angling pictures than were needed, and it was his keen eye for the human interest element that helped this volume to be better balanced, appealing to the widest possible audience.

In this manuscript I have tried to go beyond a mere descriptive account of my father's travels as they appear in the photos presented in this book. Many of the anecdotes have never been published, and I feel that the inclusion of many direct quotes from Zane Grey's own writings helps to accent the drama and excitement of the photographs. Included among these passages are some from his article about the island of Tetioroa, which are published here for the first time. Though I had read the piece many years ago, I only located a copy of it recently, along with a few of my own photographs of this most extraordinary island.

I would like to pay tribute to all the photographers represented here. To my knowledge, only two of the men — other than me — is still living. They are Frances Arledge, last of Zane Grey's personal boatmen, who lives in Russell, Bay of Islands, New Zealand; and J.E. "Aim" Morhardt who now lives in Bishop, California. Many remain nameless, but I do wish to mention those I know contributed: my brother, Romer; my brother-in-law, Bob Carney; photographers Tom Middleton, Gus and Lyle Bagnard; ZG's boatmen Peter Williams, Sid Boerstler, and Leon Warne; his brother, RC; his fishing companions, Captain Laurie Mitchell and Doc "Lone Angler" Wiborn; and secretaries, Millicent Smith, Wanda Williams, and Brownella Baker. Lastly, of course, Zane Grey himself took many of the photographs that are included here.

I would also like to give special thanks to Dr. Candace Kant for use of some of the material from her book, *Zane Grey's Arizona,* published by Northland Press in Flagstaff, Arizona, and to Dr. Joe Wheeler, now authoring a landmark biography of Zane Grey, who provided valuable sources of information and chronology for the many trips my father took during the time covered in this volume. Special thanks also for the yoeman's efforts of my loyal friend and secretary, Katharine Haggerty, who spent so many hours typing and reptyping the manuscript. I would also like to add a note of tribute to Carol Brown, to whom this book is dedicated, whose exuberance and enthusiasm about my father's writing was so contagious that it resulted in my meeting with Jim Black of Taylor Publishing Company, and the publication of this volume.

Loren Grey, Ph.D
Woodland Hills, California

The Phenomenon of Zane Grey

Photographically speaking, Zane Grey's life (1872-1939) amounts to virtually a blank page until he enrolled in the University of Pennsylvania on a baseball scholarship at the age of 20. One reason which may account for the lack of photographic records of his younger days may be that photography was then in its infancy. Even though there were many families who could afford to commission family portraits, pictures of get-togethers, and photos of their children, for whatever reason, the only known photograph taken of any family member before 1892 is a portrait of my grandfather, Lewis M. Gray; and we do not know on what date it was taken. Written records are also vague for those years and the accounts of Zane Grey's life by biographers Norris S. Schneider and Frank Gruber, who published works about my father in 1967 and 1970 respectively, leave a great many gaps about what really happened during the early years.

As the reader will see, this book is primarily a chronicle of Zane Grey's adventures and extensive travels, most of which occurred after 1910 when he became successful as a writer. As such, this account will only attempt to cover some of the highlights of Zane Grey's career and to illustrate some of the previously unseen aspects of his success as a writer, as a passionate outdoorsman, and — especially in the later years — his profound affection for deep sea fishing. When we recognize that his prodigious output covered a period of just thirty seven years and did not commence until he was nearly thirty years old, perhaps we will see that there were two Zane Greys. The first is still something of an enigma; the second, a modern Ulysses who roamed the world in an effort to fulfill his two great passions, writing and the quest for the illusive, mighty game fish.

Indeed, not only was his output prodigious, but his success has been unparalleled among writers of his generation. In all, Zane Grey wrote a total of 64 novels, 12 full-length non-fiction outdoor books, 4 boys books, 2 novel-length baseball stories, and a total of more than 250 shorter works including novelettes, short stories, and hunting and fishing and conservation articles. In all, a total of 108 full-length volumes have been published to date, more than 20 of which

have emerged since 1972. Most of the latter include material previously published either in book form or in magazines. However, two brand new volumes have appeared with material never before published in any form whatsoever. These are, *The Reef Girl,* his novel of Tahiti, written in 1936 and published by Harper and Row in 1977, and *Tales From a Fisherman's Log,* the story of his fishing adventures in New Zealand in 1927, published by Hodder & Stoughton in New Zealand in 1978.

More than 130 million copies of his books have been sold. They have been translated into 23 different languages and have undergone so many different printings, reprintings, translations, and retranslations that it is impossible to catalog them all. What is interesting, but not so surprising, is that the books continue to increase in popularity each year. The great majority of the volumes mentioned here are still in print in one form or another — either in paperback, hardcover trade edition, or large print. It is generally accepted that the image of the West as it is known throughout the world today was primarily one created by Zane Grey. His popularity has persisted in spite of the fact that, with very few exceptions, most of the so-called literary critics have either dismissed him as being too superficial and one-sided in his characterizations, or simply as being unrealistic in his characterizations of the West and the people who lived there.

Recently, even scholars have begun to awaken to the fact that there is a great deal more to his writing than is immediately apparent. Some of the quotations taken from his writings will help in counterpoint, to capture the drama in some of the photographs, perhaps even more compelling when strengthened through his words.

One theme does run not only throughout his early life but also throughout his successes and his writings as well. This was his love of the out-of-doors. Some of this he may have acquired from his father, Dr. Lewis M. Gray, who before he became a practicing dentist was a farmer, a backwoods hunter and fisherman, and a lay preacher. Some of it may also have come from his pioneer heritage, from his mother, Alice

Josephine Zane, whose great-great-great-grandfather was Colenel Ebenezer Zane, who commanded Fort Henry during two battles of the Revolution and then went West to found the city of Zanesville, Ohio. Colonel Zane's exploits, along with those of his sister, Betty Zane, as well as his brothers and the mysterious scout and Indian hunter of great repute, Louis Wetzel (whom the Indians had named "Death Wind" because of his cunning as a woodsman and his success against them with his long black rifle) formed the basis for Zane Grey's first three novels, *Betty Zane, Spirit of the Border,* and *The Last Trail.*

How did all of this come about? Perhaps no one can really explain it. In my belief, Zane Grey was a primitive genius, much the same as George Gershwin and Scott Joplin in music, and Grandma Moses in art. Grandma Moses did not become famous until she started painting at the age of 78. George Gershwin, though extraordinarily successful as a musical comedy and song writer, did not achieve immortality as a genuine classical composer until, as if by accident, he was asked to write a semi-classical piece of music based on a jazz theme to be introduced at a concert on jazz given by Paul Whiteman at Carnegie Hall in 1926. That one composition, *Rhapsody in Blue,* stamped Gershwin as the first authentic musical genius to adapt jazz themes into what was genuinely classical music. Perhaps the same can be said for Zane Grey by virtue of what he wrote about the places he saw — the grandeur, the beauty, the isolation, the openness, the vastness, the stark harsh reality of the out-of-doors — described as compellingly and poetically as has ever been done in words.

PART ONE

THE WESTERN YEARS

Early Influences
(1872-1905)

He was born Pearl Zane Gray, the fourth of five children, two girls and three boys, on January 31, 1872. Of the five children, only four survived — the oldest, Ella, passed away at the age of seventeen of some mysterious ailment, the nature of which is not known, even today. According to Professor Joe Wheeler, who is now writing the definitive biography of Zane Grey, Ella's death was a great blow to her father. The oldest boy, Ellsworth, was the rebel and at seventeen ran away from home to join the Marines. Ultimately his father settled upon Pearl as the son most likely to follow in his footsteps as a dentist. However, as a boy, Pearl was not eager to join his father's profession. During his earliest days at school, he always preferred hunting and fishing and swimming in the old rivers near their home to classwork. Most of his teachers felt he "would not amount to much." But, whereas Ellsworth had actually rebelled against his father's stern discipline, by the time Pearl graduated from grammar school at fifteen, he had reluctantly accepted his father's admonishment to go to work as a dental assistant in his lab. But Pearl never failed to spend most of his spare time romping in the woods and fishing.

During those days, Pearl developed another avocation which was to prove extremely valuable in later years. He was adept at playing baseball, particularly as a pitcher. He used to tell me that the reason he became so good at throwing a baseball was that the only way he could counter his older brother Ellsworth's bullying tactics was to throw rocks at him. He finally became so accurate that Ellsworth eventually left him alone. (Pearl's younger brother, Romer Carl, idolized him and also became proficient in baseball.) This ultimately led Pearl to a baseball scholarship at the University of Pennsylvania, where he became a star on the varsity team.

There was also another influence on his early life that may have been far more profound than anyone has yet realized. This was his association with an elderly recluse and fisherman whom the townspeople of Zanesville called "Old Muddy Miser." The friendship took roots when Pearl and Romer Carl (known as RC) got into a fight with what passed for a gang in that era, headed by the Graves brothers. Pearl found them throwing rocks at the old man who was fishing in a stream near Zanesville. Pearl saved the old man from further injury by beating up Harry, the leader of the Graves gang. After the others had gone, the old man approached him and mentioned to him that he had known his father many years before when the elder Gray had been doing his own fishing and hunting. Pearl soon found out that the old man was not only kindly, but well-educated; it was he who fired Pearl's imagination with tales of monster saltwater fish that inhabited the seven seas, which very few people had learned to catch. Although there is no evidence that the old man ever wrote anything himself, he could have stimulated Pearl's interest in writing. Certainly his efforts inculcating the love of the wild, of conservation, of fishing, played a significant role in his development as a writer and was incalculable in its effect. Even though Pearl's relationship with Old Muddy Miser ended when the family moved to Columbus, Ohio, because of financial difficulties, Pearl never forgot the frail old man whose imagination had so stirred him.

When he went to the University of Pennsylvania on a baseball scholarship, Pearl still had to provide for his room and board and pay for his books. He was offered a job waiting on tables, which he declined, then he accepted a job ushering at a local theatre. Once he had the opportunity to prove himself during the first baseball year, his pitching prowess was unexcelled. Then came the disastrous blow. The National League decided to move the pitching mound back an additional 10 feet and this was too much for his arm to handle. But because of his hitting ability, he was moved to the outfield. Pearl still had an outstanding career as an outfielder for the rest of his college career. He was looked up to by the other athletes and was made a member of the Sigma Nu Fraternity.

This portrait of the novelist's father, Lewis M. Gray, was made in Columbus, Ohio, likely around the turn of the century, though the exact date is unknown. (Right) ZG's mother, Alice Josephine Gray, with the infant Loren, around 1916.

The Brothers Gray were a strong and resourceful group. This solemn portrait shows Zane, left, with Romer Carl, seated, and Ellsworth at right. For the rest of their lives ZG and RC were ardent fishing companions.

Graduation from the University of Pennsylvania in 1896. His education hardly prepared him for his later career.

Ultimately, it was his baseball scholarship that got Grey through college; by all accounts, his pitching and batting were exceptional.

However, Pearl was essentially a loner, and because he did not drink he was not at home at the social gatherings where there was a great deal of drinking among the college students. Also, his grades, though acceptable, were poor. He did not understand mathematics and was bored with his other subjects as well. He was only at home in the library, where he read mostly stories of adventure and excitement and was fascinated by authors such as Stevenson and Melville. In the final analysis it was really his success at baseball that got him through college.

After graduation he went to New York and set up his dental practice under the name of P. Zane Grey. He had changed the "Gray" to "Grey" at that time. His first practice was adequate, but he was not happy with it. Finally, he joined the New Jersey Athletic Club, where he and his brother RC played baseball. Also, he and RC would take frequent weekend trips together, particularly to the Delaware River. In the summers, when RC was making as much as $600 per month playing baseball, they stayed at the Delaware House, a resort on the Jersey side directly across from the tiny hamlet of Lackawaxen. One day while paddling along the river in a canoe, the brothers saw three girls who were camping on the opposite side of the river. One of them was Lina Elise Roth, who was 17 years old and a student at New York Normal School, which later became Hunter College. She was studying to be a teacher. He nicknamed her "Dolly" and she called him "Doc," and this was to last throughout their entire lifetimes. He was struck not only by her beauty but by her intellect. She was studying to be a teacher and eventually went on to obtain her Master's Degree at Teachers College, Columbia University, where she studied under John Dewey and Edward L. Thorndike. And Dolly saw something in this handsome, enigmatic young man that went far beyond his dynamic good looks and the fact that he was extremely popular with women. She was the one who eventually encouraged him to quit his dental practice to become a full-time writer. From that first flirtation, came a relationship that was to last five years before they would marry in 1905.

In 1902, in his dingy flat in New York City, Pearl Grey had completed his first novel, *Betty Zane*. One of the most interesting aspects of this book is that he not only wrote it but also drew the illustrations himself. Unfortunately, no one would publish it. Finally, using money that he borrowed from Dolly, Pearl had the book printed at his own expense. Eventually, the Charles Frances Press paid for a second printing, but it did not sell well. However, encouraged by this modest beginning, he wrote two more novels, *Spirit of the Border* and *The Last Trail*, both being about the Zanes and the violent warfare of the early days of the Revolutionary War. Though the books found a publisher, they did not sell well either. Strangely enough, though it was Dolly who had encouraged him to become a full-time writer on the strength of these first three efforts, years later when it came time to renew the copyrights of these books, she failed to do so because she did not believe they would have the success his later novels had enjoyed. Ironically, since 1979, four editions of *Betty Zane* have appeared, published by different paperback houses, as well as two or three each of the other two books. The Zane Grey organization also receives royalties for these works from foreign sources.

Though it is apparent that these titles never did sell as well as his later books, when the time came that Zane (as he was to call himself henceforth) and Dolly decided to marry, they were convinced that he should quit his dental practice to devote full time to his writing, even in the face of the obvious lack of financial success they had so far endured. With the help of some money from RC, who had recently married a wealthy woman named Reba, they purchased a five-acre tract at the confluence of the Lackawaxen and Delaware Rivers, which had on it a fairly large two-story cottage.

Zane and Dolly were married on November 21, 1905 and their honeymoon commenced at the Grand Canyon and ended in California, where they toured San Diego, Catalina Island, ending up in San Francisco before returning home.

On their return, ZG quit his dental practice for good and he and Dolly moved into the Lackawaxen home. However, success still eluded him. Though he published a number of magazine stories on fishing and now had three novels that had appeared in print, sales of his books were slow and discouraging.

Canoeing with Lina Elise Roth on the Delaware River where they met. After their marriage they were known simply as Dolly and Doc.

(Above) ZG and Dolly on an outing in Pennsylvania before their marriage. (Right) This dreamy, Victorian-style portrait shows Dolly fishing near Lackawaxen around 1905.

The Grey home on the Delaware River assumed almost epic importance in the Zane Grey legend, for it was here that he wrote his first important stories, experienced his first failures, and dedicated himself completely to his writing. And the river at the door offered tranquility and an opportunity to indulge his other great passion, fishing. This shot was taken by ZG himself with a 1903 Kodak Panorama Camera.

(Left) *The house at Lackawaxen, Pennsylvania was ZG and Dolly's first home, purchased with money loaned by his brother, Romer, and Romer's wife, Reba.* (Right) *Seen from the banks of the Delaware River, the Delaware House provided a peaceful retreat for the author during his first serious writing sessions.*

By the time he and Dolly settled into their first cottage and their "rustic" way of life, ZG had already lived and worked in New York City, then retired from his dental practice with Dolly's encouragement to become, as this picture suggests, an aspiring author.

His eventual success came as a result of a chance meeting with J.C. Jones, better known as "Buffalo" Jones, who had been a buffalo hunter in the 1870s, a game warden at Yellowstone, and in later years an ardent champion of the buffalo, which had been threatened with extinction. ZG was invited by his friend, Alva James, to attend Buffalo Jones' lecture concerning the hybridization of buffalo and black cattle. Jones was hoping to breed an animal with tender meat but also capable of subsisting on the desert grasses. However, Jones' lecture was not well received. His stories were considered too farfetched; some of the audience even hooted and called him a liar. But ZG was impressed. Afterwards, he went up and introduced himself to Jones and after showing him a copy of *Betty Zane,* convinced the old man that he wanted to go West with him. Jones had conceived a new project — roping wild mountain lions to sell to zoos. He invited ZG to go with him and this was the beginning of the Western experiences — the details of which are described in a later section — that led to the publication of his first two successful novels.

Perhaps a little should be mentioned about his difficulty even after he had returned from his trips to Arizona, with his suitcase full of notes, burning with enthusiasm. His next book was not a novel; it was the story of Buffalo Jones and was called, *The Last of the Plainsmen.* It was published in 1908 by the A.H. McClurg Co. because Harper and Brothers, again, had rejected it. However, his next effort was the novel, *Heritage of the Desert,* and this time it was awarded with the famous Harper blue contract.

Ironically enough, his second novel, when finished in 1912, was also taken to Duneka, the Chief Editor at Harpers, and was rejected. ZG was crushed — this was the end of what seemed to be such a promising career. However, he had a friend named Dan Murphy, who was the husband of the poet Edwin Markham's sister, and was also a literary agent who had sold a number of ZG's outdoor stories to magazines. Murphy knew the wife of the publisher of Harpers and persuaded ZG to let him take a copy of this second novel to her. He suggested that if she liked it, to have her husband read it and then perhaps there would be a second consideration by Harpers. That is exactly what happened. Duneka was told to publish it and the book, *Riders of the Purple Sage,* went on to become the all-time bestseller, considered by many to be the most famous Western of all time. These two books were to launch ZG's fabulously successful career. It was also the beginning of the pictorial record of his travels and adventures, which follow in the subsequent chapters.

J. C. "Buffalo" Jones was as much a showman as a Wild West explorer. One of his lectures in the East capturerd ZG's imagination and it took little convincing for the old man to agree to take the young writer along on his next adventure — hunting lions in the Grand Canyon.

The incredible landscapes of the West, like these stark chimneys rising from the desert floor in Monument Valley, were a powerful inspiration to the young writer. One of the hallmarks of his mature writing is a compelling sense of place and sensitive descriptions of the scenery of the West.

The Open
(1910-1930)

As has been mentioned before, ZG was an outdoorsman long before he became a writer. But in beginning what we are calling the Western segment of this photo-journal, it seems altogether fitting to describe what the outdoors meant to him — particularly the West and how it affected his writing — by looking at his own words.

WHAT THE OPEN MEANS TO ME: Places inspire me in some sense as they did Stevenson. I love wild canyons — dry, fragrant, stone-walled, with their green-chocked niches and gold-tipped ramparts. I love to get high on a promontory and gaze for hours out over a vast open desert reach, lonely and grand, with its far flung distances and its colors — I love the great pine and the spruce forests, with their spicy tang and dreamy peace and murmuring streams and wild creatures. The Grand Canyon appalled and depressed, yet exalted me. Never yet have I attempted to write of it as I hope to. The lonely, white, winding shore line of Long Key, a coral islet in Florida, always inspired me to write. I have wandered there many profitable hours. San Clemente Island in the Pacific calls and calls me to come again to its bleak black bluffs; its tawny wild-oats slopes; its bare desert heights; its white wreathed rocks and crawling curves of surf; its haunting sound of the restless and eternal sea; its lofty crags where the eagles nest; and its almost inaccessible ledges where wild goats sleep; its canyons of silence and loneliness. Death Valley is a place to face one's soul — aloof, terrible, desolate, the naked iron-riven earth showing its travail. The sage slopes of the Painted Desert is the place for the purple that is the most beautiful of colors. Among features of nature I love color best. All of which is to say that my romances are simply the expression of my feeling for places.

It is not surprising that compelling descriptions, such as both this and those in his novels and nonfiction works, were of places that he had actually visited and seen, which had a profound effect on the nature of his books and the characters about whom he wrote. He or various members of his expeditions photographed most of these scenic vistas as well. But unfortunately, except for the representative photographs reproduced here, the majority of the pictures that were taken in those earlier days between 1910 and 1930 were greater in their number than in their quality. Those reproduced here, in a sense tell their own story. They also reveal to us how the image he created of the West, which the whole world has accepted as uniquely American, comes not only from the reality of what he saw but the marvelous imagination he displayed in describing it.

The Grand Canyon

Using the last of Dolly's savings and borrowing money from RC, ZG eagerly set out on his first great Odyssey. It was on this journey that ZG began to learn about the hardships that frontiersmen experienced: riding for days on end through the searing heat of the desert, sleeping on the ground during icy, cold nights on the north rim of the Grand Canyon, eating the meager camp food that was the traditional fare of the outdoorsman. The pain, the exhaustion, the toil, the lack of civilized amenities: these were vividly described in a number of his works such as *The Dude Ranger, The Rainbow Trail,* and others. It was also on this first journey to the West that he began to meet some of the characters he would bring to life so vividly in his books. His description of the members of his party on one of these trips is, itself, a reflection of how he saw these men and the part they played in the building of the West.

The members of my party harmoniously fitted the scene. Buffalo Jones, burly-shouldered, bronzed-face, and grim, proved in his appearance what a lifetime on the plains could make of a man. Emmett was a Mormon, a massively built grey-bearded son of the desert; he had lived his life on it; he had conquered it and in his falcon eyes shone all its fire and freedom. Ranger Jim Owens had the wiry, supple body and careless, tidy garb of the cowboy, and the watchful gaze, quiet face and locked lips of the frontiersman. The fourth member was a Navajo Indian, a copper-skinned, raven-haired, beady-eyed desert savage.

For example, Jim Emmett would fashion the character of the Mormon patriarch, August Naab, in ZG's first successful novel, *Heritage of the Desert.* Naab was, in essence, the Godfather of the clan that lived in the fertile valley the Navajos called the "Garden of Eschtah" on the banks of the mighty Colorado River, north of the Grand Canyon. Besides Buffalo Jones, Ranger Jim Owens and the Navajo Indian, both mentioned above, became prototypes for some of the characters who inhabited his earlier novels. There is little doubt that Jones and Emmett introduced him to the harsh realities of survival in the desert, as well as how they had learned to cope with the fear, the loneliness, the dangers, and the unremitting struggle to survive in this wilderness. From these experiences came several other great novels: *Desert Gold, The Light of Western Stars, Wanderer of the Wasteland,* and *Stairs of Sand.*

The Rainbow Bridge

Though he returned to the Grand Canyon a number of times after these early visits, ZG was never able to recapture the same kinds of feeling toward the land that he had cherished with Jones and Emmett until he met John Wetherill and his wife, Louisa, who had managed a trading post since 1906 on the Navajo Reservation east of the Grand Canyon. They represented yet another type of frontier settler — those who had pioneered the vast stretch of desert and mountains constituting the Reservation at that time. While Jones and Emmett harbored little but contempt for the Indian, both John and Louisa Wetherill were truly compassionate and deeply concerned human beings who cared a great deal about how the greedy and corrupt traders, Indian agents, and missionaries were exploiting the Indians on the Reservation. John and Louisa are depicted as the Withers in

the novel, *The Vanishing American.* In fact, Louisa was so revered by the Indians that she had been made an honorary member of the Navajo tribe, something that had never before happened to a white man, much less a woman. Tales of their own experiences and some of the legends about the Indians that they had learned struck a responsive chord in ZG's soul, particularly because he, himself, saw how the Indian had been treated in the Ohio River Valley as well as on any other lands that the white man had coveted in the West. This he had recounted in his first three novels, *Betty Zane, Spirit of the Border,* and *The Last Trail.*

Perhaps the culminating result of his encounter with the Wetherills was *The Vanishing American,* first published in the magazine, *Ladies' Home Journal,* in 1922. It is considered by many to be the finest and most revealing novel ever written about the plight of the Indian in the Southwest. But there was another adventure the Wetherills had related to him that fired ZG's imagination as greatly as anything since his first trip West: their having visited Nonnezochie, the mighty natural bridge of red stone that was located in Utah just a few miles north of the Arizona border. The Indians regarded Nonnezochie as a god. Of course, ZG was immediately determined to go there.

John Wetherill had been a member of the first government-sponsored party to reach the Bridge, in 1909, headed by Dr. Byron Cummings, a professor from the University of Utah. The guide who had led the Cummings/Wetherill expedition to the Bridge was a Piute Indian named Nasja Begay. The photograph on page 37 which shows Begay sitting on a rock with ZG, is itself part of the lore that now surrounds this great edifice. To my knowledge, it is the only existing close-up of this Indian. In fact, I stumbled on the original negative myself, only by accident. While casually reading the original story of the Wetherill/Cummings expedition to the Bridge in a recent issue of *National Parks Magazine,* I noticed that there was a photo cut of the Indian's head on the lower left-hand corner of the article's first page. The caption read, "Courtesy of the National Archives." The picture seemed familiar, but it was not until I had gone through ZG's book, *Tales of Lonely Trails,* looking for other material, that I accidentally stumbled onto the same photograph. However, it was misplaced in the book, positioned nowhere near ZG's description of his first visit to the Bridge. In a section near the end of the book, the caption under the photo reads, "Which was the Piute?"

Five years after the picture was taken, Begay perished during the terrible influenza epidemic that took the lives of more than 3,000 Indians on the Reservation. However, his immortality is assured not only by

ZG was among the very first to see Arizona's famed Rainbow Bridge. His Piute guide, Nasja Begay, had also led the first explorers to the site in 1909.

Grey was astonished by the giant barrel cactus, just one of which held enough water for a whole party of travelers.

this photograph but by a plaque affixed to a stone near the Rainbow Bridge telling of his part in leading the first white men there.

When ZG first suggested visiting the Bridge, Wetherill was quite reluctant to undertake such a strenuous journey. He was not sure how well an Easterner could survive the rigors of this savage uninhabitable land. There were no trails. A considerable part of the trek had to be made over a section of smooth granite mountains which the frontiersmen there had named "The Slick Rocks." ZG felt this was much too prosaic a title so he later renamed them "The Glass Mountains."

The trip would take many days, first across the vast desolation of Monument Valley to the Segi (a place ZG had named "Deception Pass," which figured prominently in the climax of *Riders of the Purple Sage);* by the ruins of Betatakin (an abandoned prehistoric Indian village first discovered by the Cummings expedition); then around the great bulge of Navajo Mountain, up over the treacherous rocks of the Glass Mountains, and down into the canyon which Nasja Begay called Nonnezochie Boco. ZG's pleadings finally won Wetherill over, and the party embarked, with Nasja Begay and Al Doyle as guides, in May of 1913.

Perhaps we should let ZG, himself, describe some of the endless hours of toil and misery, as well as the inspiring result, they endured before they finally reached their destination.

Down and down we toiled. And now the streambed was bare of boulders and the banks of earth. The floods that had rolled down that canyon had here borne away every loose thing. All the floor, in places, was bare red and white stone, polished, glistening, slippery, affording treacherous foothold. And the time came when Wetherill abandoned the streambed to take to the rock-strewn and cactus-covered ledges above.

The canyon widened ahead into a great ragged iron-lined amphitheatre, and then apparently turned abruptly at right angles. Sunset rimmed the walls.

I had been tired for a long time and now I began to limp and lag. I wondered what on earth would make Wetherill and the Indians tired. It was with great pleasure that I observed the giant Joe Lee plodding slowly along. And when I glanced behind at my straggling party it was with both admiration for their gameness and glee for their dishevelled and weary appearance. Finally I got so that all I could do was to drag myself onward with eyes down on the rough ground. In this way I kept on until I heard Wetherill call

me. He had stopped — was waiting for me. The dark and silent Indian stood beside him, looking down the canyon.

I saw past the vast jutting wall that had obstructed my view. A mile beyond, all was bright with the colors of sunset, and spanning the canyon in the graceful shape and beautiful hues of the rainbow was a magnificent natural bridge.

"Nonnezoshe," said Wetherill, simply.

This rainbow bridge was the one great natural phenomenon, the one grand spectacle which I had ever seen that did not at first give vague disappointment, a confounding of reality, a disenchantment of contrast with what the mind had conceived.

But this thing was glorious. It absolutely silenced me. My body and brain, weary and dull from the toil of travel, received a singular and revivifying freshness. I had a strange, mystic perception that this rosy-hued, tremendous arch of stone was a goal I had failed to reach in some former life, but had now found. Here was a rainbow magnified even beyond dreams, a thing not transparent and ethereal, but solidified, a work of ages, sweeping up majestically from the red walls, its iris-hued arch against the blue sky.

This was the revision of an article that ZG wrote for *Recreation Magazine,* first published in 1915, and which later appeared in his book, *Tales of Lonely Trails.* Another passage in the book reflects some of his feelings about the relationship of the Indian Guide, whom he had renamed Nas Ta Bega, and the great stone arch. He also simplified the name of the Bridge to Nonnezoshe, the name it is popularly called today.

It was then that I became aware of the presence of Nas Ta Bega. Dark, silent, statuesque, with inscrutable face uplifted, with all that was spiritual of the Indian suggested by a sombre and tranquil knowledge of his place there, he represented to me that which a solitary figure of human life represents in a great painting. Nonnezoshe needed life, wild life, life of its millions of years — and here stood the dark and silent Indian.

Long afterward I walked there alone, to and fro, under the bridge. The moon had long since crossed the streak of star-fired blue above, and the canyon was black in shadow. At times a current of wind, with all the strangeness of that strange country in its moan, rushed through the great stone arch. At other times there was silence such as I imagined might have dwelt deep in the center of the earth. And again an owl hooted, and the sound was nameless. It had a mocking echo. An echo of night, silence, gloom, melancholy, death, age, eternity!

The Indian lay asleep with his dark face upturned, and the other sleepers lay calm and white in the starlight. I seemed to see in them the meaning of life and the past — the illimitable train of faces that had shone under the stars. There was something nameless in that canyon, and whether or not it was what the Indian embodied in the great Nonnezoshe, or the life of the present, or the death of the ages, or the nature so magnificently manifested in those silent, dreaming, waiting walls — the truth was that there was spirit.

I did sleep a few hours under Nonnezoshe, and when I awoke the tip of the arch was losing its cold darkness and beginning to shine. The sun had just risen high enough over some low break in the wall to reach the bridge. I watched. Slowly, in wondrous transformation, the gold and blue and rose and pink and purple blended their hues, softly, mistily, cloudily, until once more the arch was a rainbow.

I realized that long before life had evolved upon the earth this bridge had spread its grand arch from wall to wall, black and mystic at night, transparent and rosy in the sunrise, at sunset a flaming curve lined against the heavens. When the race of man had passed it would perhaps stand there still. It was not for many eyes to see. The tourist, the leisurely traveller, the comfort-loving motorist would never behold it. Only by toil, sweat, endurance and pain could any man ever look at Nonnezoshe. It seemed well to realize that the great things of life had to be earned. Nonnezoshe would always be alone, grand, silent, beautiful, unintelligible; and as such I bade it a mute, reverent farewell.

Perhaps it is ironic that today one can take a leisurely 50-mile boat trip from Wahweap Marina near Page, Arizona, on Lake Powell, and land within an easy quarter-mile walk to the great Bridge. Now, thousands of tourists visit it every year. I have seen Nonnezoshe twice myself. Somehow I still feel deeply that I was no less awed at my first view of this great edifice than my father was when he first beheld it. But somehow his description of its wonders and the part it played in his novel, the sequel to *Riders of the Purple Sage, The Rainbow Trail,* illuminates the mystic significance of this great natural treasure in a way that has never been done before or since. In his later novel, *The Vanishing American,* the Bridge was also to play a significant role in the conflict between the primitive and the more modern religious beliefs of Nophaie, the Indian hero.

The trip west with Buffalo Jones netted a collection of live lions and handsome pelts, like the one at right.

Grey described him as, "a Mormon, a massively built grey-bearded son of the desert . . . in his falcon eyes shone all its fire and freedom." Jim Emmett, who accompanied ZG and Jones on their expedition, helped introduce the writer to life, and survival, in the wilds.

ZG, left, inspects Navajo blankets with John Wetherill at the trading post near Kayenta, Arizona, on the Navajo Reservation. The Wetherills were true friends of the Indians at a time when it was not the custom.

His keen powers of observation recorded every detail of his visits among the Indians, and later he built upon what he had seen and heard from the Indians in creating and re-creating his legends of the West.

*The Arizona badlands were a lesson in
contrasts, from the pristine sand dunes near
Yuma to the gorges and draws in Piute Canyon.*

Pioneers had called them the Slick Rocks, obstacles to all travelers who passed this way. Put off by so prosaic a name, ZG dubbed them "The Glass Mountains."

Zane Grey took this shot, at left, of the caverns and cliffs of the Glass Mountains. Below, standing before the Ruins of Betatakin, at Navajo National Monument.

The terrain, which varied from difficult to impossible, was forbidding for all but the intrepid and had helped to preserve the secrecy of the party's destination.

Coming off the trail toward the Rainbow Bridge, ZG had grown tired and weary from the ride, but remained expectant.

This was Zane Grey's first view of Rainbow Bridge from the South — a view which suddenly removed all his weariness and anxiety.

*To take it all in, ZG sat for a long time
before the monument and reflected
upon the process of its creation, the
ages and revolutions it had survived,
and the primitive eyes that had gazed
upon it in wonder.*

The Tonto Basin

It was a quest for material for yet another novel that eventually led ZG to a beautiful, pine-forested valley at the foot of the Mogollon Rim in North Central Arizona, which eventually became the center of his operations for more than eleven years, from 1918 to 1929 — the Tonto Basin. In contrast to the stark desolation of Monument Valley and the Navajo Reservation or the searing, cactus-choked wastes of the southern deserts, here was a country that an outdoorsman, a hunter and fisherman, could revel in. The top of the rim, as well as the land around its base, was heavily forested with Ponderosa Pine, Oak, Fir, and Aspen trees. The climate was relatively cool in the summer with spectacular snowfalls during the winter. Deer, mountain lions, bear, and wild turkey abounded in this sparsely settled wilderness and the streams were full of fighting trout. (On his fourth visit there in 1920, ZG commissioned Al "Babe" Haught and his brother John, a pioneer family who had settled in the Tonto Basin in 1897, to build a lodge on a three-acre spot near the foot of the rim. This was to be his Arizona home for the next eight years.)

ZG's first visit to the Tonto Basin country was in 1918, ostensibly to hunt bear and wild turkey, but really to attempt to find out the details of the bloody Graham/Tewkesbury feud which had erupted in Pleasant Valley on the northeastern portion of the Basin a generation before. ZG had heard two different versions of this feud — one from Al Doyle and another from Harry Adams, a rancher in New Mexico who had once lived in the Tonto Basin. With ZG was his brother RC, my brother Romer, and ZG's secretary, Elma Schwartz. Al Doyle was his guide and George Takahashi his cook. ZG and Doyle also hired Babe Haught and his three sons to work for them on this first trip.

ZG was enchanted with the beauty of the landscape. The accounts of his hunting successes in the basin on the rim led to a series of articles which were published in *Country Gentleman* and several other Eastern magazines of the day. Eventually, he put together many of these articles as well as his other experiences in visiting the Rainbow Bridge, Colorado, and Death Valley, to produce the non-fiction volume, *Tales of Lonely Trails,* which was first published in 1922. This trip was also important and a source of great satisfaction to him for another reason. He had brought Romer with him for the first time. As he mentioned in the beginning of the article, he was concerned as to whether Romer was old enough to take such a trip.

This start of my hunt in Arizona, September 24, 1918, was particularly momentous because I had brought my boy Romer with me for his first trip into the wilds.

It may be that the boy was too young for such an undertaking. His mother feared he would be injured; his teachers presaged his utter ruin; his old nurse, with whom he waged war until he was free of her, averred that the best it could do for him would be to show what kind of stuff he was made of. His uncle RC was stoutly in favor of taking him. I believe the balance fell in Romer's favor when I remembered my own boyhood. As a youngster of three I had babbled of 'bars an' buffers', and woven fantastic and marvelous tales of fiction about my imagined adventures — a habit, alas, I have never yet outgrown.

Anyway, we only made six miles travel on this September 24th, and Romer was with us.

Indeed he was omnipresent. His keen, eager joy communicated itself to me. Once he rode up along side me and said: "Dad, that's great, but I'd rather do like Buck Duane." The boy had read all of my books, in spite of parent and teachers, and he knew them by heart, and invariably liked the outlaws and gunmen best of all.

As it turned out, his fears concerning Romer were groundless. Even at age nine, Romer proved to be an excellent horseman and as avid a hunter as his father. The trip was a rousing success except for one fact — those who had lived in the Tonto Basin and Pleasant Valley during the time of the feud were unwilling to talk about it.

Undaunted, ZG returned to the Tonto country the next fall, in 1919, but still could not gain the information he sought. Finally, on his third visit in 1920, the residents decided he was sincere about what he wanted to write about the feud and they eagerly volunteered a great many conflicting stories about what had actually happened. The cause of that brief, bloody encounter has never really been ascertained. At the end of it, every male Graham was killed and only one Tewkesbury lived to tell the tale, and he was obviously very reluctant to talk about it at all. But from this came one of ZG's greatest novels, *To the Last Man.* It was as accurate an account of the feud as could have been obtained under the circumstances. Perhaps the only obvious bit of fictionalizing may have been that the last surviving male member of the one clan fell in love with and married a girl from the other. But the book was an instant success and has been considered to be one of his finest major historical accounts of the West.

Once his lodge was completed in the Tonto, ZG visited every year except 1928. My sister Betty went with him on one or two of those trips. Although by that time I was considered "old enough" to go, I preferred fishing at Catalina Island with my pal, Johnny Vitalich, and didn't make the trip.

As these years passed, ZG began to see that more and more settlers were crowding into the country, that the wilderness he had learned to love so much was rapidly beginning to vanish. His last visit to the Tonto Basin occurred in the fall of 1929. During that trip an incident took place that caused him finally to leave Arizona forever. This party included both Romer and Betty; photographer Bob Carney (who was Betty's fiancé); a secretary named Mildred Smith; my mother's cousin, Lillian Wilhelm, an artist; and George Takahashi. They had visited a number of places in Utah and Northern Arizona and had completed another expedition to the Rainbow Bridge to obtain added footage for a film that was being made of *The Rainbow Trail*. When ZG returned to the Tonto for his bear hunt, part of which was to be the subject of a film he was making, he found that the game laws had been changed and it was no longer legal to hunt bear during the time he wished to shoot the film. He applied for a special resident license to hunt what he called "pig-killing bears" near his lodge. During this time he met with Tom McCullough, a Flagstaff man and the resident Game Commissioner. McCullough transmitted his message to the Arizona Game Commission in Phoenix, but somehow it may have become garbled and his request was turned down. A sensational publicity event was generated as a result in which members of the media took both sides in the controversy. ZG was so angered by the way in which the whole matter had been treated that in his last visit to Arizona he wrote a letter to the Flagstaff newspaper, *The Coconino Sun*, stating flatly that he would never return to Arizona, a vow that he kept except for one brief visit to the Arizona side of the Boulder Dam in 1932. Although the incident was unfortunate, it also represented something of a pattern that ZG had developed during his life — that of walking away from a situation he did not find to his liking.

However, Zane Grey's influence on Arizona and its effects on him would prove incalculable. In the years since his first trip there as an aspiring young writer with "Buffalo" Jones in 1907, until 1930, when he was probably the wealthiest author who ever lived, we remember now not so much the bitterness the incident aroused, but the enormous output of fiction and non-fiction that came from his pen during those years. More than half of his novels and many of his shorter works, as well as outdoor articles, emanated from Arizona. Books such as *Under the Tonto Rim, Sunset Pass, Arizona Ames, The Drift Fence, The Hash Knife Outfit,* and *30,000 on the Hoof* all had their base in the Mogollon or "Tonto Rim" (as he renamed it) country.

Other than his disenchantment with the way Arizona was becoming — at least to him — overpopulated, and the above reported incident, ZG was broadening his horizons. His interest was turning more and more to deep sea fishing. In fact, fishing was ultimately to become his ruling passion. By 1930, he had already made visits to Mexico, New Zealand, and Tahiti, and his travels were to continue.

The Rogue River

Although the Rogue River is uniquely part of the American West, ZG's first interest in it was running its treacherous rapids, searching for the elusive steelhead trout that ascend upriver through the wilderness areas during the summer months (as do the salmon) to spawn in its numerous tributary streams and river head waters. Steelhead are stronger than the salmon, feed in the river, and unlike the Pacific salmon who die after spawning, return from the ocean to spawn sometimes as many as three times. They are among the greatest fighting fish that anglers yearn to tangle with. ZG's Rogue River experience was a love affair. Though unfortunately short-lived, it produced some great outdoor stories and at least one highly successful novel, *Rogue River Feud*. How the Rogue influenced him may be seen in his own description of the river when he first saw it:

Deep and dark green, swift and clear, icy cold and as pure as the snows from which it sprang, the river had its source in the mountain under Crater Lake. It was a river at its birth; and it glided away through the Oregon forest, with hurrying momentum, as if eager to begin the long leap down through the Siskiyous. The giant firs shaded it; the deer drank from it; the little blackbacked trout rose greedily to floating flies. And in sunlit glades, where the woods lightened, the wild lilac bloomed in its marvelous profusion of color, white and purple, and pink, scenting the warm drowsy air with sweet fragrance.

Then suddenly, with gurgling roar, the river performed a strange antic. It sank underground to reappear far below, bursting from a great dark hole at the head of a gorge and sliding down in glancing green inclines that ended in silvery cascades. Below Prospect the river tumbled off the mountain in mellow thundering music, to meet its main branch, and proud with added strength and beauty, it raced away between its timbered banks down the miles to the sheltered valley, through Burnham's Ranch, and by Gold Hill, slowing in a long still reach that ended in Savage Rapids. Then on to Pierce Riffle, and skirting Grant's Pass, the river twisted and chafed and fought its way through Hell Gate, and rushing over the Alameda rocks, and the ledges of the Argo Mine, it entered the canyoned wilderness of the Coast Range.

Long before the towering crags above Horseshoe Bend looked down upon the hurrying green and white stream, it had grown to superb maturity, and flowed on, here with brooding peace and there with eddying poise, yet ever and oftener breaking into fierce rapids, down into the thundering cauldron of Reamy Falls and through the Plowshare, a white furrow in the mighty boulders, and over the constricted Graves Creek Rapid.

Tyee Bar and Russian Bar and China Bar, where the miners had washed away the sand for gold, and shed their blood and left their strange graces, made wide curves for the river. It raced and eddied by turns; it tarried under the high golden meadows that shone like jewels on the black mountain slopes, it glided on in glancing ripples around Winkle Bar, gentle and reluctant and sweetly vagrant, as if to lull and deceive, only to bellow sudden rage at the confines of Blossom Bar, and to prepare itself for a sullen surrender to treacherous Mule Creek Canyon. When it emerged from that barrow black-walled crack it was a subdued and chastened river, yet glad to be free once more, and to receive graciously The Amber brook that tumbled off the mossy cliffs on to the winding beauty of Solitude, where the black firs encroached to the water's edge, and the sun shone only at midday down upon the ledged and barred river, and the wild ducks played among the reeds, and the weird and lonely water ouzels built their mud nests under the overhanging rocks, and the eagles screamed aloft, and the deer and bear made trails along the shores. But at last the leaps of Clay Hill and Two Mile Rapids released the river from the hundred-mile grip of the mountains.

Here it opened out and slowed down and spread wide over shallow gravelly bars, and ran on merrily, its fury spent, its mood changed, its age realized, on through the pastoral country of the coast, past the picturesque farms of the Indians and the rude shacks of the fishermen, broadening the meandering, smiling from its shiny pebbled bed at the retreating banks and the low colorful hills, and so on down to Gold Beach, assuming a deep, calm majesty when it found its home in the infinite sea.

ZG first learned of steelhead fishing in the Rogue River through a Mr. Lester, a salmon fisherman from Long Key, Florida, but he was not able to make his first visit there until 1916. At that time the fishing run was excellent on the Rogue, but he caught no steelhead. Then, in 1925 he decided to explore the mysterious and fascinating primitive area which extended from Graves Creek near South Pass more than 35 miles down the river to Illahe, about 20 miles from the Rogue's mouth. The only way to reach this part of the river was to take a horseback or walking trail or to run it by boats. It was during this first run down the Rogue that ZG first discovered Winkle Bar. His description of how he acquired the property and what it meant to him is given here.

On my never-to-be forgotten trip down the Rogue we had camped on the canyon above Winkle Bar, and I have reveled in my first sight of this beautiful isolated spot.

The rushing river at this point makes a deep bend round a long oval bar, with rocky banks and high level benches above, and both wooded and open land. Here it flows through a lonely valley set down amid the lofty green mountain slopes. A government trail winds out some twenty miles to the nearest settlement. Far indeed is it across the dark Oregon peaks to railroad or automobile road!

We tarried at Winkle Bar a few days, far too long if one ever hoped to be free again of its beauty and solitude and its wonderful fishing. But I rather invited being chained by that memory. And this summer I had bought Winkle Bar from the native prospector who held it on a mining claim; and all through the long restless days of our swordfishing on the Pacific I had dreamed of the verdant green, the murmuring river, the stillness and sweetness of that Oregon fastness.

ZG, himself, took a hand in helping to build the main cabin and some of the smaller lean-tos on Winkle Bar. I remember because this was my first visit to the Rogue and my first attempt at catching a steelhead. It was an exciting and successful summer of fishing for everybody but me. However, there was one episode my father wrote about so touchingly in his book, *Tales of Fresh Water Fishing,* which I have never forgotten. This is when I despaired of ever catching a steelhead after my friend Gus had already landed one. My father agreed to take me fishing by myself and help me catch a steelhead. Though I never did land one on that trip, it was a singularly touching experience for me and it was written so beautifully that it remains something of a classic. It was the only time in my life when I had my father to myself, alone, without someone else being around.

Days passed without Loren catching a single steelhead. In his desperation he went to using a spinner, and then grasshoppers. It was fun to see him chase them, but I disapproved of his bait fishing.

"But dog-gone it, dad I read where President Coolidge fished for trout with worms!" he protested stoutly.

"True, Loren, he did, and got himself criticized by a lot of highbrow fly fishermen who think it disgraceful to use bait. Don't misunderstand me, Loren," I replied, earnestly. "I've seldom used anything but flies here on the Rogue, but in my own brook in Sullivan County, New York, I used to fish with worms. We couldn't catch trout there with anything else. It's no disgrace to catch a fish on anything, so long as the tackle is right and you do it fairly. But in your case I want you to practice casting with a fly."

"Well, I'm not stuck on it," said Loren, glumly. "Here I've cast flies for six days. *Six Days!* and no fish . . . Then you saw me snag myself in the seat of the pants. *And you laughed!*"

"Loren, boy, I couldn't help it," I replied, apologetically. "You were so funny."

"Huh! Say, if you want me to practice casting, why don't you take me fishing?" he queried, seeing he had me in a corner.

"All right, son, I'll do it. Tomorrow! All day!"

"Down to Missouri Bar?"

"Yes. We'll start early so as to get there first." He whooped and ran around like a lunatic, and pestered all of us for tackle.

Next morning bright and early we were off. I would have preferred it dark and lowering, for sunny days are not good on the Rogue. We climbed to the Gold Beach trail, and went down, with Loren ahead, manifestly content.

Our destination was a mile below camp. We crossed the river in our skiff, and began to fish. I let Loren go ahead. Sometimes he managed to get out a good cast. But not when he saw me looking! I simply prayed for a trout to rise to his fly. But none did. Slowly we worked down the river; and in the place where the others had had such good sport neither of us had a rise. Still there was always hope and Loren seemed happy.

When lunch time came he was hungry as a bear. I had not brought much lunch, so I saved most of mine for a later hour, when I knew he would be hungry again. We went on down the river, and Loren never showed a single sign of weariness or disgust until mid-afternoon.

"Oh, heck! Can't I get a bite?"

"Lorry, a fisherman must learn to stick," I replied. We went on trying likely holes. Never a rise! I had gotten to the point of yearning to hook a trout and let Loren take the rod. It was a very vital occasion. I seemed to be on trial. But the lad had the true spirit of a fisherman. The rocks and river and mountains were sufficient. We plodded back, finding we had come miles over rough shore. Loren never complained, and he stayed with me without a falter. He had on heavy wading boots, too large for him. But no one would have guessed it from word or action. When we got back to Missouri Bar I was tired. The sun still shone hot. I sat down on the sand, with my back to a rock, while Loren went to fishing. He would not give up, though his arm was limp. I went to sleep. When I awoke he was chasing grasshoppers. It was great to watch him, for he might have been stalking big game. He would talk to them in this wise: "You yellow son of a gun! I'll assassinate you!" Then whack with his stick. Very often Loren would quote something from one of my books, as his brother Romer, at his age, had been wont to do.

I discovered presently that during my nap Loren had built an elaborate water corral. He had done this before on other occasions. Finally, he captured a grasshopper and put it on his hook. "Now I'll ketch a trout," he averred, happily. The sun went down, and it grew time for us to start back. He fished so patiently that I hated to call him. We crossed the river and climbed the steep slope to the trail. Loren again took the lead, with a good brisk step — one I found hard to imitate. He had an eye for trees, lizards, squirrels, birds. But he did not talk. Once I said, "Lorry, I'm sorry it was such a bum day."

"It wasn't bum, dad," he said, cheerfully. "You don't have to ketch a fish to have a good day!"

It was to be nine years before I would land my first steelhead, and then on the North Umpqua River, some photos of which are included in Part Two of this book.

The next year, we all descended upon the Rogue, full of high spirits and enthusiasm. I was older, better able to cast and knew I was going to catch a steelhead. But there simply were no fish. The building of the Savage Rapids Dam in 1926 resulted in great amounts of excess irrigation water being dumped back into the river, which raised the temperature higher so that the summer runs no longer materialized. The steelhead did not enter the river until the early rains came, usually in September.

But, as with all of his writings, the Rogue River is immortalized in language that has no rival. A small part of the ending from *Rogue River Feud* is reproduced here.

Beryl stood back from the edge of the bar, casting down along shore with her inimitable grace. She forgot the arrival of the pack train. She no longer heard the bells on the mules. She grew oblivious of Kevin. He, too, fell under the spell. And the river glided on in an endless solitude, its eternal song, low and musical, near at hand, droning sweet melody from the rapid at the bend, and filling the distant drowsy air with its soft thunder.

Boulder Dam

This is perhaps the only time I traveled with ZG when he went strictly to a Western locale for the purpose of obtaining material for a novel. He had been intrigued by the stories he had heard of the construction of Boulder Dam, which at that time was to be the second largest man-made edifice ever built, exceeded only in size by the Golden Gate Bridge. I remember that we first traveled to Las Vegas, where ZG spent several hours talking with the Sheriff of Clark County. We then visited the site of the dam, which was about one-third completed at the time. Ironically, the picture I took of him at the dam site was on the Arizona side and as mentioned earlier is the last time he ever was inside the State of Arizona. One of the most fascinating and exciting parts of the journey was crossing the site of the dam on a wooden platform with flimsy wooden railings suspended by cables a thousand feet above the river.

In my opinion, *Boulder Dam* is one of his most underrated novels. The narration of the exciting events that occurred in the story was a compilation of accounts he had heard about what had happened to the men who worked on the dam. More than thirty-six were killed during its construction and there were at least two men who were swept down through the diversion tunnels, only one of whom survived to tell the tale. Also as it was told, ZG's account of white slavery in Las Vegas under the mob control that existed in that day was down-played rather than exaggerated, which the Eastern critics maintained. The Sheriff of Clark County told him, at that time, that in Las Vegas *anything* went if you had money to pay for it. This may still be true of Las Vegas or any of the other Nevada cities today, only it is more hidden, and white slavery as a practice has been much reduced in scope.

Boulder Dam, though written in 1932, was in some ways ZG's epitaph of the West. He made only one more trip to collect material after that time, and that was in 1934 when he traveled to Idaho to the scene of a huge avalanche that had destroyed a village and created Reelfoot Lake. The basis of that trip was told in his novel, *Thunder Mountain.* However, the epilogue of *Boulder Dam,* in itself, may give us some pause for thought as to the future survival of man and his technological skills.

The canyon yawned there black and dark under a pale and failing sun. The wide V-shaped gap was open as it had been in the beginnings of time, after the great inland water had cut its tortured way to the sea. On the canyon walls colossal scars showed the action of a recent glacial period. Far up the canyon gleamed the pale green teeth of the retreating ice, sinister and deadly, yielding only to another age.

Below foamed and thundered the rapacious river, augmented to its old volume, no longer red but dirty white, remorseless and eternal.

Life had failed on the earth. Inscrutable nature had gone on with its work, patient, terrible and endless. A mournful wind swept across the gaunt desert, down the naked halls and shingles, across the barren flats.

But the earth, with its long past age of creation, its dreamers and builders who had passed on, was only a tiny globe in the universe. Other planets were evolving. And that divine Thing felt by Lynn in his vision had no beginning and no end. The spirit moved ever toward perfection and immortality.

Babe Haught and his wife had known the Tonto Basin since settling the area in 1897.

(Above) *ZG with cubs outside the lodge built for him by the Haughts.* (Right) *At the hunting camp with his horse, Juan Carlos.*

Performing his morning ablutions at his hunting camp in the Tonto Basin. There was a chill in the air and the water, but the tales he coaxed from the locals revealed that passions had once boiled on this ground.

From the Tonto Rim, ZG could scout the rills and canyon below for game. Even from a distance, he was an exceptional shot.

During the day he enjoyed hunting along the Tonto Rim, but he never neglected his writing, and the secretaries who accompanied him on most of his travels served many functions, from carrying firewood to preparing his manuscripts.

(Left) *George Takahashi, the writer's
longtime cook and companion, was also a
capable hunter, shown in this picture with his
own bear.* (Above) *Daughter Betty was
introduced to the wilderness at an early age
and enjoyed an occasional jaunt on Juan Carlos.*

*Among his hunting companions were Lee Doyle,
above, and Captain Laurie Mitchell, right.*

The writer's study was a gallery of souvenirs, riding tack, and memorabilia from his incredibly succsssful career as a writer and outdoorsman. Note the Swastika on some of the ornaments in the room. ZG had discovered this emblem on an Indian rug he had purchased from John Wetherill long before it became a symbol of Hitler's Nazi Germany.

This 1931 family portrait captures ZG, center, with his family.
From left are son Romer, daughter Betty, wife Dolly, and son Loren.
In the background, Betty's husband, Bob Carney, with Bob and
Betty's daughter, Michelle.

ZG's Movie
Experiences

As previously mentioned, there have been 113 full-length movies made from ZG stories. They include two from more direct sources — *Zane Grey's South Sea Adventures,* which was produced by Sol Lesser from films ZG made during his travels in the South Seas, and *White Death,* a movie that ZG himself produced in Australia. What is perhaps less well known is the active role ZG played in the filming of a considerable number of the earlier movies. The first films dealing with his books were made in 1918 and, not entirely coincidentally, this was the time he moved to California to establish a permanent home. He quickly saw that the motion picture was a medium for reaching a much wider audience — for the method, the locale, as well as the romance inherent in his novels.

ZG's first active role in a film was assisting with publicity material for *The Rainbow Trail* in 1918. Then, in association with Benjamin Hampton, he formed his own film company, Zane Grey Productions, which made no less than seven full-length motion pictures. He was concerned that the movies should follow the book faithfully, so he insisted the story, as he had written it, should be of central importance and the characters and stars who played them, secondary. However, he did not have a great deal of enthusiasm for the details of filmmaking and only became actively involved in visiting the locations of some of his films after he had bought out Hampton's share of Zane Grey Productions and sold it to Jesse Lasky. This association with Lasky resulted in the production of no less than 54 films based on his books during the period from 1922 to 1929.

His contracts with Lasky Famous Players, later known as Paramount Studios, provided a clause that the films should be shot at the location where the book had been based. He personally traveled with Lasky on a number of location trips, particularly to the Rainbow Bridge, and to many other locations described in the various books. Despite this close association, which ultimately served to make Paramount Studios

a major production company, there were no pictures of ZG and Lasky together in our files. One was sent to me by Lasky's daughter, Betty, but it was so crudely hand colored that it was not suitable for this publication. Perhaps the most notable of all the photographs we have, which were few in number where ZG was actually seen in the company of others on the movie set, was one taken of him with Richard Dix and Lois Wilson. It happens that the negatives I found, including this one, were processed by Sherman Rose, nephew of Harry Sherman who produced so many ZG movies for Paramount during the 1930s and 1940s. It was Rose who called attention to the fact that large as life, leaning against the camera, was a young man named James Wong Howe, who was to become one of the most celebrated cameramen in the early history of American films. There have been rumors — yet unsubstantiated — that the man with his face peeping out behind the camera may have been producer-director-actor, John Huston. But, I have never been able to verify this one way or the other. In addition, the director of the film, but not shown in the photograph, was Victor Fleming, who was to become a film immortal for his direction of *Gone With the Wind* some years later.

Many of these films are classics, perhaps the finest being *To the Last Man, Wanderer of the Wasteland* (one of the very first movies made in color), and *The Vanishing American* in 1925. Unfortunately, they were silent movies, and as a result, because of the changes in acting style and the lack of sound, few of them are seen today except as examples of the old movie-making techniques. Also, by 1927, when the talkies first appeared, ZG's relationship with the studios was disintegrating. The era of production moguls such as Lasky, Sam Goldwyn, Louis B. Mayer and others was approaching. They became increasingly less concerned with making movies representing ZG's portraits of the West than with promoting their own writers or stars of the moment.

The beginning of the world-wide Depression in

1929 signaled the end of ZG's participation in movie making. Despite his insistence, he was no longer able to dictate terms to the studios as to the way in which the movies were to be made. During the years of the Depression and even after his death in 1939, the filmmakers found out that they could make a Grade B movie on a cheap budget, without any name stars, and use ZG's name as the lead and make money. After the 1930s, there were only three really top grade films made from his books, and all of them were released after his death: *Western Union,* by Twentieth Century Fox in 1940; *Robbers Roost,* produced by Goldstein-Jacks in 1955; and *The Maverick Queen,* with Barbara Stanwyck, also in 1955.

Re-releases of many of the old talking movies are seen somewhat rarely on American television but extensively abroad, even to this day. However, his films were responsible for launching the careers of some of the most famous early and late screen idols in cinema history. These included such names as Tom Mix, Dustin Farmin, Richard Dix, Jack Holt, Randolph Scott, and in later years, such stars as Shirley Temple, Gary Cooper, John Wayne, Roy Rogers, and Richard Boone. Even the famous American Indian athlete, Jim Thorpe, played a role as an Indian Chief in *Wild Horse Mesa.* Of those still active in filmmaking, Barbara Stanwyck, Dean Jagger, and Robert Mitchum all played roles in leading ZG films. The stunningly successful television series, *Zane Grey Theatre,* however, brought to an end the feature length filming of the ZG movies. In the 129 sequences of this show there were more than 35 Emmy and Oscar Award nominees, and many winners — including Ernest Borgnine, David Niven, Charles Boyer, Anne Baxter, and Richard Boone, to mention only a few. *Zane Grey Theatre,* also in its last year of production, was the production vehicle for the launching of the career of one the most successful television producers in recent history — Aaron Spelling.

There is little doubt that ZG's influence on motion picture filmmaking was impressive as far as our understanding of the West is concerned — as were the novels themselves. Almost every Western motion picture ever made has elements which bear some resemblance to the image of the West Zane Grey created.

Stars Jack Holt and Sally Blaine took time out from the filming of Wild Horse Mesa *to pose with the author on the set.*

(Left) *ZG is photographed with young cameraman James Wong Howe, stars Richard Dix and Lois Wilson, and an upstart actor named John Huston, center.*
(Above) *ZG with actress Billie Dove.*

White water rapids on the Rogue River in Oregon were a challenge ZG enjoyed second only to fishing for the wily steelhead trout.

*After a day on the river, the men had
to caulk and paint the boats. (Right) ZG did
much of the work on the cabin on the
Rogue River at Winkle Bar.*

Zane Grey, Dolly, Betty and Loren posed before the cabin at Winkle Bar in 1924. Their romance for the place was enormous, and it occupied an important place in the most productive years of the writer's life.

At the house in Altadena, California, ZG kept in shape with his rowing machine in a sunny spot on the roof.

The house in Altadena was bright, airy and spacious. A new wing was added to the house, including a writer's study which could only be entered from the second story of the main house to insure his privacy while writing.

In this study, Grey was able to
surround himself with the
souvenirs, research materials,
and tranquility which he needed
to produce the works which
streamed from his fertile
imagination. The study in
Altadena became his ideal
working environment.

MOVIE EXPERIENCES / 91

In addition to the bearskins and Indian symbols in the study, the picture of Nonnezochie *over the hearth was a constant reminder of that marvelous time in Arizona.*

*When his brothers and sister visited
Altadena in 1933, Zane Grey was the most
successful novelist of all time.*

*The author's visit to the construction site of
Boulder Dam in 1932 was the last time he set foot
in Arizona.*

Injury limited his mobility in the latter years, but throughout his life he remained lean and healthy and fond of hard work outdoors.

PART TWO

TRAVELS TO THE ENDS OF THE EARTH

"So I took my rod and string of small mouthed bass and threaded the familiar tow path through the lanes toward home."

Sports Fisherman
Supreme

ZG's two consuming lifetime passions were fishing and writing. It is still not clear how early he developed his interest in writing or where it came from. Neither of his biographers to date really has had an answer for this. On the other hand, why did he not really commence writing until he was nearly thirty years old, while his love of fishing started early in his boyhood? Possibly, his love of the outdoors could have been a form of rebellion against the stern discipline of his father, and an ascent to the influence of "Old Muddy Miser." Apparently, both his mother and father shared the idea that a fisherman was a "lazy, bad boy grown up, never helping his mother, who stays away all day and is never home for supper. He always carries a bottle. You've seen drunken men. Well, that's what fishing and a bottle does." The lesson of the bottle, which was also reinforced by his father's abstinence, apparently was successful because ZG never took a drink of alcohol in his life. But fishing remained a much-loved avocation in his early years and was to become an obsession that occupied most of his later years.

The photographs in this section are centered around these outdoor interests and reveal a side of him with which most of his Western readers are not familiar. Perhaps an irony is that the photographs in this section are of much better quality and more spectacular than those of the Western travels. Of course, there are logical reasons for this. One of the most important is that the art of photography was not as highly developed in the years between 1907 and 1920 as when he commenced his more extensive foreign travels after 1925. Whether fortunately or unfortunately, photographs of giant, leaping marlin or of landing huge gamefish or spectacular trout are simply more visually exciting than a treed lion or a pack train traversing the deserts or mountains. Still, the ardent fisherman will find these photos more exciting and intriguing than will those who are not familiar with the sport.

ZG's successes and failures in deep sea fishing also led to the development of much heavier tackle than any which had been used previously. There is little doubt that his pioneer efforts laid the foundation for what is virtually the science of deep sea fishing today. At the same time, there are other aspects to his travels reflected in the photography as well: his tenacity and determination, and the persistence with which he pursued his quarry, a success that no angler before or since has matched.

By 1937, which was the year of his first serious illness, Zane Grey held 10 All-Tackle World Records for large gamefish, including the first marlin swordfish over a thousand pounds ever landed on rod and reel. Very few of his most exciting experiences, as well as his thoughts concerning the encroachment of commercialism and population on the natural wonders he beheld, failed to be recorded either in books or in the articles he published in many different magazines.

The first story he ever published was in *Recreation Magazine* in 1902 and was a fishing yarn called "A Day on the Delaware." Two photographs reproduced here are from that early era.

Perhaps another reason why this aspect of his career is less known is because, though he wrote a total of ten fishing books, they were mostly detailing his triumphs and failures and personal experiences, and had appeal only for the die-hard angler. Today, because the emphasis on fishing is so much of the *how-to* variety, the tales of a person's experiences in his own angling successes and failures, no matter how exciting, are not very popular. But during all this time, after he became immensely wealthy and could indulge himself in almost anything he chose, writing still occupied the major part of his time; he never neglected it, even during the last two years of his life. On nearly every fishing day he would awaken at dawn and write for an hour before going out. If the weather was bad, he would sit in his tent or cabin and write all day long. Many of his Westerns were written in these fishing camps, and a number of them were written on

ocean liners going to and from California to places such as Tahiti, New Zealand, or Australia. Instead of socializing with guests on the cruise or participating in games and activities, he would shut himself up in his cabin after breakfast and write. He made it a practice during most of his literary career not to eat lunch, as a way of preventing himself from becoming overweight. That, with his exercise on the rowing machine and strenous calisthenics, kept him in superb physical condition for most of his life.

Florida

Although ZG ventured extensively beyond his home grounds of Ohio, Pennsylvania and New York, his early travels were mostly non-fishing trips — one to Tampico and the Yucatan, Mexico resulted in a highly exciting adventure story entitled "Down an Unknown Jungle River," and a boy's book entitled *Ken Ward in the Jungle*. His honeymoon odyssey with Dolly included a visit to the Grand Canyon, traveling on to Los Angeles and San Diego, and even some fishing at Coronado where he caught a shark off the pier. This was also the occasion of his first visit to Catalina Island, which was later to become one of his favorite fishing haunts. Interestingly, that year he and Dolly stopped at San Francisco less than two months before the great earthquake of May 13, 1906 which destroyed most of the city.

It was not until 1910 that ZG took another extensive trip and this was his first full-fledged fishing excursion to Long Key, Florida, part of a long string of tiny coral islets that extends almost like a necklace from the tip of Florida to Key West. It was here that he caught his first sailfish, a rare permit, one of the elusive gamefish to be found in those waters. It was here also that he discovered the wily bonefish.

Aficionados of the sport of fishing will argue at great length about which are the greatest, most elusive, most difficult gamefish to land. Though there are no statistics by which to measure this, some fishermen will rank alongside the mighty blue marlin and yellowfin tuna three much smaller species of the Pacific steelhead, the Atlantic salmon and, last but not least, the bonefish. At this writing, the world record for bonefish is only a little over 16 pounds. This rascal inhabits the coral flats and tropical shallows of waters all over the world, usually at depths of only two to six feet. He is bright, silvery-white in color, which makes him almost invisible against the blinding white grains of fine coral sand covering these areas for several miles at a time in some locations. He is named the bonefish because he has no teeth but rather two bony plates on the upper and lower portions of his mouth. His head and mouth somewhat resemble that of the fresh water sucker. These plates are used to crush the shells of small crustaceans, such as crabs and mussels, which are his principal source of food. For sheer power, on an 8 to 20 pound test line with appropriate tackle to match, his speed and stamina are awesome. In the days that ZG fished for bonefish, fishing was done with bait. In modern times it has been discovered that bonefish will also take a fly, so fly fishing tackle similar in size to that used for steelhead, Atlantic salmon, or trout is usually the custom.

ZG managed to visit Long Key for a few days or even weeks at a time over a period of fourteen years, sandwiching his visits in between trips to Catalina, Mexico, and his Western junkets. However, in the fall of 1924 a huge hurricane struck Long Key, wiping the entire island and all of the habitations off, down to the bare coral. After hearing of this, ZG was so disheartened that he never returned to Florida again.

Of course, his experiences with bonefish resulted in a series of articles published in magazines and again in one of his fishing books, *Tales of Fishes*. Also, he wrote one of his best fictionalized articles, a satire called "The Bonefish Brigade," from his Florida experiences. At the time it was written, he was president of Long Key Fishing Camp. The story is about the almost paranoid secrecy and strange habits of the members of this club, which they displayed in their efforts to capture a record bonefish. The article was first published in the *Izaac Walton League Monthly Magazine* and an offprint of it was made, which ZG used to give his various friends as a Christmas present. This story was also reprinted in the anthology, *Zane Grey Outdoorsman*, published by Prentice-Hall in 1972. For a number of years, the bonefish ZG caught, seen in the photograph on page 189, was the record for the Long Key fraternity (at least according to ZG's story), until one of his fishing buddies finally produced what appeared to be a heavier one, which proved to have been somewhat garnished with a series of sinkers put into the fish's stomach before it was weighed. Whether all of this actually took place is only conjecture, but it made for one of the most entertaining and humorous stories ZG ever wrote.

For Grey, fishing was an art, a sport,
a sublime recreation.

*Stream fishing in Ohio, ZG
practiced what he had learned
from "Old Muddy Miser."*

*Years later, when he came to Florida,
he was able to net his catch, a rare
permit, on the coral shoals off Long Key.*

Long Key was a combination holiday retreat and fishing camp. After a hard day's fishing, they could still dress for dinner.

*Loren and Betty with one of their
father's secretaries at Avalon
Bay, around 1921.*

*Rowing ashore in the launch, ZG's party
stops off for an outing on the island.*

The Gladiator was a seaworthy yacht with a specially rigged crow's nest and fishing chair.

From the crow's nest, a keen eye could spot fish ahead. Here, ZG has just caught sight of a broadbill.

When word got back that the author had tied into a mammoth broadbill, a crowd gathered at the dock for a glimpse of the catch. This shot was taken in 1926.

This very unusual shot shows ZG's 1,000-pound broadbill leaping in his angry struggle against the line. Broadbill of this size almost never leap from the water.

Catalina Island

During his honeymoon with Dolly, as related earlier, ZG visited Catalina for the first time. Though it was February (that is before the regular fishing season begins), he was so intrigued by the island's quaint charm and its aura — what amounted to that of a tiny fishing village despite its being less than 26 miles from the busy port of Los Angeles — that he resolved to come back. His first visit there to fish after his honeymoon was in July of 1914, the year before I was born. It was during this time that ZG and Dolly were considering leaving the East for good and settling in California. In July of 1918, they rented a house at Avalon with the thought of being there indefinitely. The first trip, ZG contented himself with catching halibut and white sea bass from a row boat in the middle of Avalon Bay, but soon he moved on to larger game. At the time, one of the premier established fishing associations in the world was the famous Tuna Club, which had been founded by Charles Frederick Holder in 1912. After finally catching his first 100 pound tuna, a great gamefish that abounded in the waters around Catalina, ZG became eligible and joined the Club and was ultimately elected vice-president. From there he graduated to one of the most spectacular gamefish of all the seas, the striped marlin. He and his brother, RC, established a record by catching and releasing twelve marlin in one day off San Clemente Island, some 18 miles southeast of Catalina.

Soon his interest turned to a much more challenging foe, the mighty broadbill swordfish. The broadbill probably should also be ranked with the blue marlin and yellowfin tuna as one of the mightiest and fiercest fighters of all gamefish. At the time, using the primitive tackle that was then available, and using a line that, by Tuna Club standards, could not hold more than 72 pounds wet, many anglers had hooked and fought these giants, but few had been landed.

After a remarkable encounter with a huge swordfish, which is documented here by what I judge to be one of the greatest broadbill jumping photographs of all time, ZG began to realize the true challenge of bringing in the broadbill. He also recognized that the tackle he was using was inadequate for the task. This account is even more significant because hooked broadbill rarely leap. In the estimation of both RC and ZG and the boatman, this fish would have weighed well over a thousand pounds.

As it happened, RC, who was ZG's favorite fishing companion, had yet to catch a broadbill, whereas ZG had landed one over 400 pounds. So, it was RC who was manning the tackle that day when they sighted their quarry. Of course, they had no idea what they were in for. The fish looked large, but they did not realize how huge he was until he commenced a series of fantastic leaps. In those days, in order to hook a broadbill it was necessary to find one surfacing the water and then feed him a bait. It has only been discovered in the last few years that broadbill feed in deep water and only come up to the surface to sun themselves. This one apparently was not that well-fed because he quickly snapped up RC's bait and for five and one-half hours RC labored with his small Murphy rod and undersized reel and line, which was only adequate for striped marlin. Finally, when the weather turned rough and RC became seasick, he decided he could no longer handle the fish, so he turned the rod over to ZG.

When ZG took the rod he was certain that he was going to subdue this fish in short order, but the broadbill had stopped leaping and was just moving along 200 to 300 feet under the surface. After three and one-half strenuous hours, Thad Murphey, the boatman, suggested that he take over and so, reluctantly, ZG relinquished the rod because the chance of an individual record was no longer possible since more than one angler had already fought the fish. After three more hours, Thad also became tired so ZG pulled on the rod while Thad wound the reel. In the meantime it had become dark. The rest of this encounter must be left to ZG's own descriptions, as it was published first in *Tales of Swordfish and Tuna* in 1925 and later in *Zane Grey Outdoorsman* in 1972.

The two of us working together, began to tell on the swordfish. We stopped him. We turned him. We got him coming. Still we could not tell how close we had him. The 150-foot mark had worn off the line. Then just when our hopes began to mount and we began to believe that we could whip him, the reel went out of gear. The drag refused to stick. Dan could wind in the line, but there was no drag to hold it. He had to hold it with his thumbs. This was heartbreaking. Yet we seemed to rise to a frenzy and worked all the harder.

At eleven o'clock, in spite of our handicap, we had the swordfish coming again. It looked as if we had the best of him. Eleven and one-half hours! It did seem as if victory would crown our combined efforts. But we were both well-nigh exhausted and had to finish him quickly if we were to do it at all. The sea was dark now. A wan starlight did not help us, and we could not always tell just where our quarry was. Suddenly, to our amazement, he jerked the line from under Dan's thumbs and made a magnificent run. Then the line slacked. "He's off!" exclaimed Dan. I told him to wind. He did so, getting nearly all the line back. Then the old strain showed again on the rod. Our broadbill had only changed his tactics. He made some sounding thumps on the surface. "Say, I don't like this," said Dan. "He's runnin' wild."

I was reminded that Boschen, Adams, and myself all agreed on the theory that broadbill swordfish wake up and become fierce and dangerous after dark. This one certainly verified that theory. In the dark we could not tell where he was, whether he was close or near, whether he menaced us or not. Some of the splashes he made sounded angry and close. I expected to hear a crash at any moment. Captain Dan and I were loath to cut the line; stirred and roused as we were, it was difficult to give in. We took the chance that as long as our propeller turned the swordfish would not ram us.

But if we had only known what we were soon to learn, we might have spared ourselves further toil and dread.

Suddenly the line began to whiz off the reel. This time the fish took off several hundred feet, then stopped. The line slacked. Dan wound up the slack, and then the fish jerked out more. Still he did not run. I let go of the rod and raised myself to look out into the gloom. I could just make out the pale obscurity of heaving sea, wan and mysterious under the starlight. I heard splashes.

"Listen, Dan," I called. "What do you make of that? He's on the surface."

Captain Dan relaxed a little and listened. Then I heard more splashes, the angry swirl of water violently disturbed, the familiar swishing sound. Then followed a heavy thump. After that soft, light splashes came from the darkness here and there. I heard the rush of light bodies in the air. Then a skittering splash, right near the boat, showed us where a flying fish had ended his flight.

"Dan! Flying fish! All around us — in the air!" I cried.

We listened again, to be rewarded by practically the same sounds. Captain Dan rested the rod on the gunwale, pointing it straight out where we heard the swordfish. *Snap!* Then he wound in the slack line.

"There!" he boomed, as he dropped the rod and waved his big hands. "So you know what that broadbill is doin' out there? He's feedin' on flyin' fish. He got hungry an' thought he'd feed up a little. Never knew he was hooked . . . Eleven hour an' a half — an' he goes to feedin'! . . . By gosh! If that ain't the limit!"

It was long after midnight when we reached the island. Quite a crowd of fishermen and others interested waited for us at the pier, and heard our story with disappointment and wonder. Some of our angler friends made light of the swordfish stunts, especially the one of his chasing flying fish after being fought for more than eleven hours. It did seem strange, improbable. But I had learned that there were stranger possibilities than this in connection with the life and habits of the denizens of the deep. I shall always be positive of the enormous size of this broadbill, and that, after being fought for half a day, and while still hooked, he began chasing flying fish.

This incredible battle finally had convinced ZG that he needed heavier tackle; stronger lines and better rods were essential for these great fish. So, he petitioned the Tuna Club to create a special class of line of 36 strand with approximately 108 pound test and rods and reels to match. Until that time, most of the broadbill hooked had broken their tackle. Many of them had died dragging these large amounts of the customary 72 pound test strand line down behind them after breaking it. However, despite his pleadings and support from some other anglers, the Board of Directors of the Tuna Club turned him down. As a result ZG reverted to what was his pattern — he quit the Club. But in this case he did not leave Catalina. He commissioned J.A. Coxe, who was then one of the most famous reel makers, to build a reel for him that would hold more than 500 yards of the new, heavier line. The Shaver Rod Company created a rod appropriate to the stronger line. ZG also had built a fifty foot fishing launch which he named the *Gladiator* and which had a special crow's nest attached to the mast in which he could guide the boat and hook a fish.

Zane Grey with world record broadbill caught off Catalina Island in 1926. The one he landed weighed in at 582 pounds.

He realized that the broadbill, being not overly hungry when he was sunning himself on the surface, would shy away if he saw a leader or line attached to the bait, so the task was to feed a bait to him without the fish seeing the line or leader.

With this new tackle and the special boat, ZG and RC set a record for capturing broadbill that has never been excelled. During the years between 1921 and 1927, usually not fishing more than a month or six weeks at a time, they landed 36 broadbills, all of weights over 300 pounds. In July of 1926, ZG capped his record with the capture of a 582-pound, world record broadbill. Just three weeks later, RC beat his record with one of 588 pounds.

In the meantime, ZG had first thought of spending the winters as well as the summers in Catalina, but he quickly realized that the cool breezes of summertime turned into cold, blustery winds during the winter. I remember spending half a semester of first grade in the Avalon schools, but then we moved back to Los Angeles, ultimately settling in Altadena near the foot of the majestic Sierra Madre Mountains north of Pasadena. The original house we had occupied, halfway up the slope on the north hillside, was no longer by itself. Buildings were springing up everywhere. As an added irritant, Tom Mix had built a house just directly below ours. On the roof, Mix had a large circle with an "M" painted on it. Whether or not this was deliberately designed to incite ZG's wrath or was just Mix's way of publicizing himself, we never figured out.

Finally, in 1924 ZG commissioned the building of his famous adobe-style house on the highest point of land overlooking the bay on the north side. That house is now a hotel called the Zane Grey Manor. (On one of my recent visits, the owner said he decided to put a second story on the house and learned that my father had been told by the Indians in Arizona that if one mixes goat milk with the adobe, it would make construction much stronger. So the concrete was mixed with goat's milk. It proved to be so strong that the second story was built without any need of additional bracing.)

As with many of the places ZG visited and publicized, civilization was encroaching, and what had once been placid Avalon now became a tourist mecca in the summertime. Many of the tourists would climb up to his house and trample over the flower gardens and pound on his window when he was writing. What was much worse, commercial harpooning of broadbill reached a point where they were no longer able to find them and ZG finally quit Avalon for good after the 1931 season.

Nova Scotia: ZG's First World Record

Although ZG's record broadbill was landed at Catalina in 1926, his first world record was actually achieved two years earlier. Upon the advice of Captain Laurie Mitchell, an Englishman who had fished extensively in Nova Scotia and Newfoundland, both for Atlantic salmon and the giant bluefin tuna that inhabit those waters, ZG finally made his expedition to Nova Scotia. He was inspired by letters written to him by Mitchell, who had lived in Liverpool and had fought between fifty and sixty of these giant tuna and had caught only one — the largest on record, 710 pounds. Many of the other anglers who had fished there had had the same result. Mitchell was convinced that the new and improved tackle that ZG had designed to fight the broadbill at Catalina Island might prove successful in subduing some of these monsters.

Shipped with him, ZG had a special launch that he had had made for Florida fishing, which was 25 feet long and equipped with two engines, the special Catalina revolving chairs, and furnished with rod sockets. To the fisherman today, of course, this equipment seems commonplace. But the pioneering efforts of ZG and the others, particularly at Catalina Island, eventually resulted in methods and equipment that would subdue enormous fish — marlin up to 1500 pounds and sharks up to 3000 pounds. Today, the rods used are of fiberglass or graphite composite and the line is primarily monofilament or Dacron. The swivel chair with the movable rod socket, the butt of the rod resting between the legs when one fights the fish, is the method that is used to subdue most of the large gamefish.

The trip proved to be an auspicious one and Captain Mitchell's predictions about the use of the more sophisticated tackle proved to be correct. On August 13th, ZG landed a 608 pound tuna, which was the second largest ever landed, the first being Mitchell's 710 pounder. Then, on August 22, he landed his 758 pound world record. On the last week of this trip he managed to fish one of the inland rivers and conquered two Atlantic salmon on flies — one a beauty of about 15 pounds. In later years when we were fishing for steelhead on the North Umpqua, I remember he used to talk incessantly about the Atlantic salmon and he was convinced that they were as great a fighter fish as steelhead. He was always making plans to go back to Nova Scotia and Newfoundland to do some more of that fishing. Unfortunately, he never made it.

ZG's Hopi Indian style home (at left) on Catalina Island.
His yacht, Fisherman I, *can be seen in the harbor*
in the background.

The living room of the Catalina home was festooned with relics and souvenirs of the writer's travels in the West.

On his Nova Scotia adventure, ZG brought
in this world-record bluefin tuna,
scaled at 758 pounds.

*In his youth, ZG had visited the Mayan ruins
in the Yucatan; that memory brought him
back time and again.*

Mexico and the Pacific

"A fisherman has many dreams, and from boyhood to manhood, one of mine was to own a beautiful white ship with sails like wings and sail into lonely tropic seas." This was ZG's opening paragraph in his book, *Tales of Fishing Virgin Seas.* In 1924, during his visit to Nova Scotia, he found the ship of his dreams. It was a large, three-masted sailing schooner that had been used primarily as a cargo vessel and she suited his purposes admirably. She was 146 ft. in length, 38 ft. in beam, and had crossed the Atlantic twice, once a record run without cargo. This maiden voyage to Mexico and the Pacific was to be the first of his pioneer deep sea expeditions, an odyssey which would later lead him to the far waters of Tahiti, the Tonga and Fiji Islands, and then eventually to New Zealand and Australia. But this first voyage on the *Fisherman,* the vessel's new name, was the most pioneering of all.

His first visit after joining the ship, which had been refitted to suit his purposes in Halifax, was Cocos Island. Cocos Island is a tiny, uninhabited chip of land some 500 miles off the shores of Costa Rica. Rumors of buried pirate treasure on this uninhabited, lonely isle have abounded for hundreds of years. There is one recorded story of a man named Keating who was reputed to have sailed away from Cocos Island and disappeared with over $100,000 worth of gold and jewels, which apparently he had stolen from his companions. No one knows whether he made it to shore or perished in the sea with his ill-gotten bounty.

Sailing through these Pacific waters, ZG's party caught many strange varieties of gamefish, including a Wahoo, which at that time was only known to be indigenous to the Atlantic Ocean. But the sharks were so ferocious and abundant that they devoured most of the gamefish before the catch could be landed.

ZG's next destination was the Galapagos, a barren cluster of volcanic islands more than 500 miles west of Ecuador, lying squarely athwart the equator. The strange iguanas, giant tortoises, and other forms of native plant and animal life had been made famous both by Charles Darwin and later the naturalist, William Beebe. Though the party found the islands fascinating, fishing was not as good as at Cocos Island, and there were also the omnipresent sharks.

After leaving the Galapagos, the *Fisherman* journeyed to the Perlas Islands, a small group of coral-fringed islets, an archipelago in the Gulf of Panama about 50 miles from Panama City. Large gamefish were still not much in evidence, so they sailed north, stopping at a small village on the mainland of Mexico, located on a landlocked bay named Zihuatanejo. Here, gamefish of all sizes and shapes and species were in abundance. They landed many sailfish, including another world record, a 135 pound Pacific Sailfish. ZG had an exhausting four-hour battle with a giant black marlin before finally losing him. The last stop on this journey was Cabo San Lucas, which in those days was a tiny, primitive fishing village, now, of course, one of the most famous and prominent resorts for big gamefishing on the Pacific. Here, ZG landed another world record tuna, and wrote of it:

Soon after letting out my line I saw a flash of silver and a swirl behind my feather jig. A cracking smash, making a huge patch of white water, was followed by a terrific lunge on my line. It jerked me out of my seat. Despite the grip I had on my rod I almost lost it.

The tuna shot along the surface, between two green furrows, showing a broad back, and as he went he surely gathered headway. I yelled for Sid to chase him. That became the most spectacular surface run I ever saw. It was incredibly swift. My reel shrieked as the line shot off. A remarkable feature also was the length of line out of water. Fully one hundred yards! Beyond that stretched two hundred yards more, whipping the water white, as the tuna dragged it in a curve over the surface. He had four hundred yards out, and for a considerable number of moments before we began to gain. We chased him some distance before he sounded.

Then I settled down to a grueling contest. The depth at which the tuna worked added much to my difficulties. For two hours I labored hard and persistently before I made any obvious impressions on him. He was heavy and tireless No doubt about the punishment he inflicted upon me. But at last I got him to the surface, where the size elicited yells from all of us. He turned head down and dove. As he gathered momentum my reel began to shower me with spray. In a few seconds he took off half of my line. That with the drag on! When I had to release the drag I bade him good-bye. After one thousand feet he slowed up. But he went on down until he had reached a depth of thirteen hundred feet. When he stopped I endeavored to lift him. Not an inch! Harder I pulled. Presently the dead weight slightly moved and I recovered a fraction of line. I had to lift with all my strength. But that was not very great now, as I had overworked. Excitement and hope revived me, and I strained every muscle. The time came when I could lift him and gain several feet of line; and of course the farther up I got him the less the tremendous strain. In what seemed an age I lifted him to the surface, a blazing blue and yellow monster. It took both boatmen and Captain Mitchell to haul this tuna into the launch. The magnificent flaming colors, blue, gold, silver, opal, pink, bronze, changed marvelously every second, and were most strikingly beautiful as he quivered and died. This tuna measured nearly seven feet in length and over four in girth. He weighed three hundred and eighteen pounds.

What is most interesting about this giant is that ZG never realized during his lifetime that this was yet another world record that he had added to his collection. (It was not recorded by the IGFA because it was captured long before records of that sort were kept.) This remarkable tuna was a world record until 1981 when an angler off one of the long range fishing boats from San Diego landed one of 387 pounds. The chronicles of this voyage fill the pages of the book, *Tales of Fishing Virgin Seas*, which was published by Harpers in 1925.

New Zealand: The Angler's Eldorado

It was not long after ZG's return from his Mexican odyssey that he received a letter, urging him to undertake a new fishing adventure, from a gentleman named C. Alma Baker, who lived in Russell, Bay of Islands, New Zealand. Baker regaled him with stories of huge gamefish of every description — striped and giant black marlin, ferocious mako and thresher sharks, and a great variety of smaller gamefish as well. Baker also stated that the New Zealand government was very interested in providing some help in defraying some of the trip's expenses, as they were eager to publicize their angling riches. This fit in ideally with ZG's plans because he could still spend his summers at Catalina and Oregon. Of course, December through March in New Zealand was their summertime.

There was not time to re-outfit the *Fisherman* for so long a voyage, so ZG decided to travel by steamer instead. He left on December 25, 1925 with Captain Mitchell as his fishing partner. On the way down they stopped at Papeete, Tahiti. Here they were told by native fishermen that there were giant marlin up to thirty feet in length in the waters around Tahiti, but no one had ever dared to try and capture one. There was no time to follow up the challenge, but ZG vowed to return.

Though the town of Russell, which was more or less the fishing headquarters for Bay of Islands in picturesque New Zealand, was quite charming and reminded ZG of Avalon, he decided to make a camp of his own and he secured permission to set up his tents on Orupukupuku Island, which was farthest out toward the fishing grounds. Orupukupuku also had the advantage of having a virtually landlocked bay, Otehei, that would be protected from high winds and waves from any direction.

ZG's fishing skills, as well as his rather obvious scorn for the primitive methods of the New Zealand sportfishermen who had come before him, soon provoked controversy. Most of the New Zealanders' tackle was a variation of fresh water fly fishing rods and reels that had been developed in England, with the reel underneath the rod. The custom of trolling, that is, moving the boat at a rapid rate to keep the baits near the surface, was a custom unknown to New Zealanders. Mostly, they drift fished with live bait and captured few.

ZG's gamefish prowess, and that of his fishing partner, quickly silenced nearly everyone there except for the most vociferous critics. Between the members of their party they subdued over a hundred striped marlin, with weights up to 350 pounds. ZG landed the first broadbill swordfish ever caught in New Zealand waters; but the climax was Mitchell's capture of a giant black marlin which, after being cut into three pieces and sent to Russell for weighing, still came in at 976 pounds. Mitchell's own account of landing this huge fish tells the story.

Well, I worked harder than ever before, on any fish, even my big tuna, yet I couldn't stop the beggar. He was game, fast, incredibly strong. He would take short quick runs, down deep and high up. Once he had off almost all my line, all except thirty yards! I had been fighting him nearly four hours when he took a last short run and stopped! After that I found I could hold him, lead him, drag him. Soon I brought him up. He looked so tremendous that I was scared weak. I had not dreamed of such a fish. I nearly fell out of my chair. Bill hauled on the leader, and Warne gaffed him. Then Bill reached over with a rope and got it round the fish's tail, but not in a loop or knot. Bill fell down in the cockpit, yelling for help. Crack! went the gaff. Bang! Bang! Bang! The huge swordfish tail jarred the whole boat and half filled it with water. We were deluged. Warne got another rope and got that on the banging tail, same as Bill's. He was lifted off his feet and slammed to the floor of the cockpit. I left my rod and jumped to their aid. Then the three of us lay flat on our backs, feet braced on the gunwale, and strained every nerve and muscle to hold that fish. Morton had wit enough to grab another rope; making a noose, he threw it tight around the tail and then to one of the posts. Only when we had his tail in a noose did I recover. . . .By Gad! it was an awful fight!

ZG's own description of it, as well as his feelings about Mitchell's great catch, is also self-explanatory.

It was almost round, very fat and full clear down to the tail, and solid as a rock. Faint dark stripes showed through the black opal hue. The bill was short, and as thick as a spade handle at the point. The hook of the lower maxillary had been blunted or cut off in battle. Huge scars indented the broad sides — many of them. The length was twelve feet, eight inches; the girth six feet, two inches; the spread of tail, four feet; and the weight nine hundred and seventy-six pounds. It had to be taken to Russell and cut into three pieces in order to weigh it at all. What an unbelievable monster of the deep! What a fish! I, who had loved fish from earliest boyhood, hung round that Marlin absorbed, obsessed, entranced and sick with the deferred possibility of catching one like it for myself. How silly such hope! Could I ever expect such marvelous good luck? Yet I knew as I gazed down upon it that I would keep on trying as long as strength enough was left me. That ought to be a good many years, I figured. Oh, the madness of a fisherman! The strange something that is born, not made!

Of course, as can be seen, it aroused a fierce determination in ZG to somehow, somewhere, land a fish greater than Mitchell's! Interestingly enough, this giant black marlin, captured in 1926, is the largest of the species that has ever been landed in New Zealand waters. Off Cairnes, Australia at present, black marlin as heavy as 1376 pounds have been landed. Of course, the all time black marlin record is still the largest fish (other than sharks), caught on a rod and reel — Albert Glassell's 1560 pound black marlin monster caught off of Cabo Blanco, Peru, in 1956. Ironically, a blue marlin of over 1600 pounds was landed in 1984 off Kona, Hawaii, but unfortunately the record was nullified because the line and leader exceeded the length specified in the IGFA Standards.

A few weeks after Mitchell's catch an event occurred illustrating that sportsmanship, as well as rivalry, can exist between two fishing companions.

Pretty soon Frank called:
"They're waving on the Captain's boat."

"Sure enough," I said. "Guess he must have a strike or have seen a fish."

But when Bill appeared waving the red flag most energetically I knew something was up. It took us only a moment or two to race over to the other boat, another one for me to leap aboard her, and another to run aft to the Captain.

His face was beaming. He held his rod low. The line ran slowly and freely off his reel.

"Got a black Marlin strike for you," he said with a smile. "He hit the bait, then went off easy. . . .Take the rod!"

I was almost paralyzed for the moment, in the grip of amazement at his incredible generosity and the irresistible temptation. How could I resist? "Good Heavens!" was all I could mumble as I took his rod and plumped into his seat. What a splendid, wonderful act of sportsmanship — of friendliness! I think he realized that I would be just as happy over the opportunity to fight and capture a great black Marlin as if I had had the strike myself.

"Has he showed?" I asked breathlessly.

"Bill saw him," replied Captain.

"Hell of a buster!" ejaculated Bill.

Whereupon, with chills and thrills up my spine, I took a turn at the drag wheel and shut down with both gloved hands on the line. It grew tight. The rod curved. The strain lifted me. Out there a crash of water preceded a whirling splash. Then a short blunt beak, like the small end of a baseball bat, stuck up, followed by the black and silver head of an enormous black Marlin. Ponderously he heaved. The water fell away in waves. His head, his stubby dorsal fin, angrily spread, his great broad deep shoulders climbed out in slow wags. Then he soused back sullenly and disappeared.

"Doc, he's a monster," exclaimed Captain. "I sure am glad. I said you'd get fast to your black Marlin."

Though this fish was not as large as Mitchell's, he was certainly a great gamefish, responsible for one of the most magnificent photographs of a leaping marlin ever taken. The photograph was taken by Peter Williams, ZG's boatman, from ZG's boat while ZG was fighting the fish from Captain Mitchell's boat. He was landed, only after a grueling fight of some four and one-half hours, where he went down several hundred feet and had to be pulled up as dead weight.

After several incredibly successful weeks, which also brought another record to ZG's list — a 111-pound Pacific yellow-tail (a record only recently broken in Mexico in 1984) — the expedition headed for the Tongariro River. The Tongariro is only one of a number of magnificent rivers rushing out from New Zealand's snow-capped peaks then down to many lakes and the ocean. Except during floods it is unbelievably cold and clear. Until the turn of the century, all the New Zealand rivers were barren of fish, but around 1905 the U.S. Fish and Wildlife Service sent down to New Zealand stocks of Russian River (California) steelhead and McCloud River brown trout, as well as eggs of Chinook and Coho salmon. The steelhead eggs that were planted into the rivers became fingerlings and went down to the ocean to disappear forever. However, in the streams that ended in lakes such as Lake Taupo or Lake TeAnau, the fish remained in the lakes and then returned to the streams to spawn. The brown trout, on the other hand, not being an anadromous species in nature, lived mostly in the rivers and grew to enormous size. Even today, the rainbow and brown trout fishing in New Zealand is excellent, though the mean size of the fish has declined from an average of about 12 pounds at the time ZG visited to about four or five pounds today. The New Zealand government is now beginning to undertake stocking and replanting some of the fish because of the heavy influx of anglers who now invade New Zealand each year to partake of its celebrated fishing.

At the Tongariro there were other fishermen, but most of them seemed to concentrate near the mouth of the river, and although they caught great quantities of trout with what amounted to salmon tackle, ZG soon found a camp several miles up the river near what has now become one of the most famous stretches of the Tongariro River — the Dreadnaught Pool. ZG landed his first Tongariro trout here which weighed eleven and one-half pounds. Ironically enough, the best fishing seemed to be at night, where the procedure was to strip off line some distance down the stream and then wind it back. On the wind back, they would receive a strike almost every time. This extraordinarily successful trip was capped by Romer's capture of a fifteen and three-quarter pound rainbow trout, the record for the expedition that year. Perhaps ZG's description of the ending of a day on the Tongariro, relating his feelings about its special beauty and the great brown-backed, red-sided trout that thronged its icy waters, says it best.

The day, however, had begun badly for Captain Mitchell and so it ended. He could not raise a trout. Then we left the rousing fire and strode off over the boulders into the cool gathering twilight. Hoka carried two of my trout, Captain two, and Morton one. We threaded the *ti*-tree thicket and the jungle of ferns, and crossed the perilous panel in the dark, as if it had been a broad and safe bridge.

My comrades talked volubly on the way back to camp, but I was silent. I did not feel my heavy wet waders or my leaden boots. The afterglow of sunset lingered in the west, faint gold and red over the bold black range. I heard a late bird sing. The roar of the river floated up at intervals. Tongariro! What a strange beautiful high sounding name! It suited the noble river and the mountain from which it sprang. Tongariro! It was calling me. It would call me across the vast lanes and leagues of the Pacific. It would draw me back again. Beautiful green-white thundering Tongariro!

ZG was to return to New Zealand, this time with the *Fisherman* in 1927 and again in 1929. In 1929 the trip was notable because they spent several weeks at Mercury Bay, fishing for the ferocious mako shark which abounded in that part of the New Zealand waters. The mako shark is a somewhat distant cousin of the bonita shark, which inhabits the California coast. However, the New Zealand mako is much different, though the two look alike. Mako are great fighters, grow to be very large in size, and are among the few species of shark that leap after being hooked. Although many larger mako were hooked and lost at Mercury Bay, the record was Romer's 604 pounder, which was caught during the 1929 trip.

Interestingly enough, when I visited New Zealand on my third trip in 1977, I brought with me some notes of ZG's 1927 journey in a notebook, under the heading, *Tales From the Angler's Log.* I also brought an album of photographs to show to Frances Arledge, one of the last surviving of ZG's boatmen in Russell. At that time he was 72 years old. We spent two enjoyable hours reminiscing about the pictures, with him telling me many tales that went with them. They were recorded and transcribed and were to become the basis of the book, *Tales from the Fisherman's Log,* which was first published by Hodder & Stoughton in 1978. As a result of this, another New Zealand publisher wrote and asked permission to reproduce *Tales from the Angler's Eldorado,* which had first been published as a result of ZG's 1926 trip. It was suggested that we add some material that included several articles he had written about his 1929 fishing for mako sharks, as well as a number of new photos from Mercury Bay. This became the revised edition of *Tales of the Angler's Eldorado,* which was then published by Reed Publishers in Wellington in 1981.

*Zane Grey with a 19-pound Atlantic salmon
caught on an expedition to Nova Scotia.
These were wily fish that put up a good fight.*

ZG once wrote, "My childhood
dream was to have a great
white yacht with sails like wings and
sail into lonely tropic seas." When
he sailed Fisherman I to New Zealand
in 1927, he made that dream
come true.

On his visit to the Galapagos Islands, ZG was intrigued by the spiny iguanas which greeted the party on the beaches.

The writer was duly proud of his world-record 318-pound yellowfin tuna caught off Cabo San Lucas, Mexico in 1925.

Setting up camp on Otehei Bay, Bay of Islands, New Zealand in 1926 demanded some good strategy and a strong back.

*Once the tents and facilities were in place, the
members of ZG's party were ready to test
the New Zealand waters.*

*From the promontory overlooking the Bay,
the party had a spectacular view of the
islands and the striking coastal terrain.*

Although ZG had to teach the locals about his more sophisticated gear, the fishing was incredible and the size of the catches unprecedented. The writer's first broadbill brought smiles to the faces of New Zealanders Peter Williams, standing, right, and Frances Arledge.

(Above) *This is the only leaping shot of Captain Mitchell's world-record black marlin, caught in the waters off New Zealand. The fish weighed in at 976 pounds.* (Right) *The giant black was the largest all-tackle gamefish ever caught until Zane Grey landed his 1,040-pound blue marlin in 1930. But Mitchell still holds the New Zealand record, nearly 60 years later.*

New Zealander Peter Williams took this shot, one of the best ever, of ZG's 704-pound black marlin leaping in its bitter struggle against the writer's outstanding strength and tackle.

*The giant 704-pounder was the largest ZG
ever caught in these waters.*

The New Zealand fishing camp was equal to his best Hollywood sets. Here he compares notes on tackle with J. A. "Doc" Wiborn, whom he called the "Lone Angler."

Grey's tackle was as up-to-date as any in the world, and if a particular rig wasn't available, he would have it made to order. Here he checks out the day's tackle before an outing on the Fisherman II.

The mako shark is as ferocious and powerful as any monster in the sea. The razor sharp teeth on this 604-pounder, caught by Romer in Mercury Bay, indicate the danger of the fish. Grey claimed to have seen mako jump as high as fifteen feet out of the water when caught.

ZG fishing in the "Dreadnaught Pool," one of the most famous fishing holes on the Tongariro River in New Zealand. This shot was taken on the 1926 expedition.

Romer's 15-pound-8-ounce Tongariro trout was the largest ever caught on ZG's expeditions. ZG took the picture. He was equally proud of his own brace of rainbows.

On the Fisherman I, *ZG visits with an American Indian family who bear a striking resemblance to the native Maoris of New Zealand. They were part of a troupe that had come to New Zealand to promote his new film, The Vanishing American. After six months away from their Arizona Reservation, they were very homesick and eager to talk to him.*

No matter how vigorous his fishing adventures became, and no matter how long he toiled in search of his prey, Grey never neglected his writing. He would always find a time and a place to work at the craft which had made all of his adventures possible. This picture was made at his fishing camp in New Zealand in 1927.

(Above) *The camera crew shot footage from the launch as the* Fisherman I *lay at rest off Rangiroa in the Tuamotu Islands near Tahiti in 1927.* (Right) *ZG's son-in-law Bob Carney with Tom Middleton, two of his best cameramen, off New Zealand on the 1927 trip.*

Tahiti: Triumph and Tragedy

ZG was not particularly thrilled about the strenuous but unproductive fishing he had encountered at New Zealand in the Spring of 1930. He had spent five long months there, most of it encountering extremely bad weather and poor fishing. Still, he was eager to try the mysterious waters surrounding Tahiti and particularly the Tuamotu Isles, a group of more than 1,000 coral atolls and reefs that extend over a thousand miles southwesterly from a point just north of Tahiti. After unsuccessfully scouting up and down near Tahiti and Moorea for several weeks, ZG finally decided to sail to the Tuamotus. Though there was only one encounter with one of the giant marlin there, one of the most bizarre happenings in all of his years of deep sea fishing occurred near Rangiroa, the largest of the Tuamotu atolls. (A similar experience occurred to me several years later which was to convince all of us who saw it, what strange, unknown monsters still lurk in the depths of the ocean.)

A Prehistoric Monster of the Deep

Our interpreter, John Blakelock, went ashore to the village, Avatoru, and brought back some native fishermen. We interrogated them in the same manner as we had the Tahitians. They identified all the fish of which we showed photographs, except the broadbill swordfish, and they positively claimed him for Polynesian waters, averring, however, that his sword, instead of being an extension of the upper maxillary, was an extension of the lower.

This was a statement that seemed impossible to take seriously. But I was compelled to take it seriously. One of our visitors was the native governor of Rangiroa. He was intelligent and spoke English fairly well. He stuck to his statement about the swordfish with the sword underneath, and could not be shaken. The other natives were equally as positive.

This swordfish grows very large and the natives fear it. When they fish for bonito from the sail boats — trolling the same pearl-shell gigs used by Tahitians — very often the school of bonito will mass under the boat and almost cling to it. This is a sure sign one of the great swordfish is about, and when the fishermen look down they are sure to see one, and often more.

Sailfish, spearfish or marlin, tuna, wahoo, and other large fish, were often seen outside the reef. Sharks were plentiful and ran very large. The governor said some sharks were eight fathoms in length. This statement was another hard one to swallow. But we were in unknown waters, unfished by anyone except natives with the crudest of tackle and method. *Quien Sabe?* You can never tell. I, for one, believe absolutely in the fabled sea-serpent.

We put out to sea in three boats, with orders from me to hang pretty well together. Middleton, the camera man, was in the *Red,* and he was to follow us closely. We trailed two teasers behind each boat. I forgot to say that the natives caught us a few mullet for bait before we left. We trolled both bait and feather gigs; and ran around outside of the entrance to the lagoon. The sea was just a little rough for comfortable fishing, but not bad. Birds were in evidence, though not in any large numbers. We sighted no schooling fish and did not see any fins.

Peter caught a small yellowfin tuna, the same species we found off Mexico and South America, a wonderfully brilliantly colored fish, blue and silver, with yellow fins. Soon after that Peter hooked another on the feather gig.

He was hauling this up and had brought it somewhere near the boat when he let out a yell. I jumped up and instantly sighted a huge green shape looming up astern.

"Whale!" shouted Peter. As he was a whaler, I at once took his word for it.

But as the fish came closer, I saw it was not a whale, but a shark. Only in size did it resemble *Rhineodon typus,* from which fact I took it to be one of those most colossal of sharks. I was intensely thrilled and excited, but not frightened.

Frances yelled something, and Peter answered. I waved for Middleton to hurry close in the *Red* and frantically motioned that there was something to photograph.

The great fish passed astern of me, not far from the surface. He was yellow and green in color, had a square head, immense pectoral fins, and a few white spots. He was eight feet across the back, and considerably longer than my boat — conservatively between thirty five and forty feet. The after third of his body and his tail were lean compared with the bulk of his head and shoulders. He went under us, out on the other side. Just then Peter's tuna, which he had kept winding up, came into view. It passed close to the head of the shark. He did not appear to see it. Then he turned, flashed a bright blaze, and went down shining until he faded and disappeared.

He had been with us only a few seconds. When he was gone we recovered wits enough to calculate upon what we had witnessed. The eye sometimes deceives one and excitement is no help to accurate observation. But there could be no doubt that we had seen an astounding and almost incredibly huge shark.

"He was forty feet long and had more beam than our launch," declared Peter. "When I first saw him I thought he was a fin-back whale."

"Some joker, that fish!" exclaimed Frances. "No one could have made me believe it. But I saw him."

These New Zealand fishermen were used to big fish, and not given to exaggeration. So I relied much upon their judgment. And presently I figured out that the fish had not been a *Rhineodon*. He was not a harmless whale-shark, but one of the man-eating monsters of the South Pacific. Then I was more frightened than I remember being for a long time.

When I first heard my father's story about sighting this monster I was sure he had seen something like it, but I was not ready to believe that it was as huge as he claimed. As he had — albeit with tongue in cheek — admitted to me before, all fishermen were prone to exaggerate and he was no exception. Naturally, he usually denied this when referring to his own catches. Except for the relatively harmless basking shark and the equally placid *Rhineodon typus,* to our knowledge, no shark of this size or species had ever been seen before. But to me, his tale still seemed to sound like the fable of the sea serpent or the Loch Ness monster, or even a more elusive legend, just recounted, that ZG had pursued all over the South Seas — the fabled swordfish with the bill on the under jaw. Huge specimens had allegedly been seen and reported, not only by natives but by white men near the Tuamotu and Tonga Islands, though none had ever been caught or classified.

But, to use an expression ZG was fond of, I had to "eat crow!" We were returning home from our 1933 expedition, my second with him to Tahiti, on the *SS Manganui,* which had left Papeete in the early morning bound for San Francisco. At 5:00 p.m., the ship was due to pass between two of the most northwesterly of the Tuamotu atolls before its long voyage on the open ocean to California. We were all up on the deck for a last glimpse of a tropical island. The weather was unusually calm, with only a light breeze blowing off from the atoll about two miles to the east. Behind us the dark bulk of Tahiti could still be seen low on the horizon with its inevitable shroud of white cumulus clouds. I was on deck above my dad — although I did not know where he was at the time — chatting with the ship's physician and a couple of other passengers. With me also, was my Catalina fishing pal, Johnny Vitalich. I saw a small flock of birds wheeling and circling almost directly ahead of the liner, usually an indication of tuna or bonito chasing schools of small bait. As the liner moved majestically towards them I also noticed a huge yellow patch in the water which appeared to me, at the time, to be a school of small fish bunched up very close together. I was somewhat mystified by the yellow color. As the ship passed closer, John and I went to the rail to look and were utterly stunned by what we saw. I first thought it was a whale, but when the great brown tail rose in the ship's wake out of the water as the fish moved ponderously away from the liner I knew immediately that it was a monstrous shark. The huge round head appeared to be at least ten to twelve feet across if not more. The back of the fish was covered with hundreds of white spots, which when we came close enough I saw were actually barnacles. We were all nearly too awed to speak. It was indeed the same shark that Dad had told about sighting several years earlier — or else one just like it. Rangiroa, the atoll near where Dad saw his huge specimen five years before was only about a hundred miles southeast of here, so it was possible it could have been the same fish.

Finally, Johnny and I found our voices and yelled and pointed and the other passengers crowded to the rail. I saw that Dad was on deck below me, peering down in the water, as overwhelmed as I. In the grip of such excitement, estimates of size are often inaccurate, but it was my belief that this huge yellowish, barnacled creature must have been at least forty or fifty feet long. The other passengers, including the ship's physician, were as dumbfounded as we were at the shark's incredible size.

What we had seen was something that no ichthyologist had ever dreamed existed. Sadly enough, no one had a camera handy to record this monster on film. The largest known species of this type of shark — generally known as a sand shark or black tipped shark — had hardly been known to exceed a length of about 15 feet.

Of course, the questions that raced through my mind then and have excited me ever since are still unanswered. Obviously, he must have been very old, if for no other reason than the barnacles that covered his back. What kind of creatures did he feed upon? The birds that followed him must have had reason to suspect that he would lead them to schools of small fish. But how could he chase them down with his huge bulk? He was not a whale shark; the whale shark has a distinctive white purplish green appearance with large brown spots and a much narrower head and body. So what was he — perhaps a true prehistoric monster of the deep?

Not more than a few moments after Johnny and I and the other passengers had expressed our amazement, Dad burst up the stairway to our deck. "Did you see it, did you see it?" he almost shouted, his face and eyes aglow.

"Wow! I certainly did!" I said, in great excitement. "I think he was even bigger than the one you saw at Rangiroa. And I have to admit I didn't really think the one you saw was that big — you made a believer out of me!"

"Son, you'll learn that your Dad never exaggerates," he said in mock solemnity. "But I sure made you eat crow!"

I had to admit he was right. Someday I'm going down there again and try to get a hook into one of those monsters — and perhaps even an underbilled swordfish — and settle the matter of how big they *really* are, once and for all!

It was also at Rangiroa where Captain Mitchell, who ZG used to say was "the luckiest fisherman alive," hooked the first giant marlin about which the natives had so often told ZG. When he saw how long the fish had been on, and how large it was, ZG finally was invited by Mitchell to come aboard his boat to help him get a closer look at the great swordfish itself. It was truly enormous. They estimated that it was at least 18 feet long. It was so large that it could not leap clear of the water, the greatest marlin they had ever seen. But Mitchell's tackle was inadequate to the task. Finally, his rod broke and although they were able to get the leader up and fasten it to one of ZG's heavier rods, the line that was on ZG's rod was not wet (the old linen lines were much stronger when wet than when dry.) The marlin sounded down to about 1500 feet, died there and broke the line of its own weight. Though they had ended up using ZG's heaviest tackle, ZG had begun to wonder whether even this much larger equipment was adequate to try and land such an enormous quarry. It was then that he resolved he would build rods and reels that would be large enough to accommodate any fish ever hooked.

After many more days of uneventful fishing, in which they landed only one small marlin, the *Fisherman* sailed for Apataki, another small atoll further south, without much significant result. So they returned to Tahiti and then to the islands of Raiatea, Tahaa, and the strikingly beautiful Bora Bora, the most northwesterly of the inhabited Society Island chain. ZG then trolled around Bora Bora, the Raiatea, then finally back to Tahiti.

While fishing down around the southern part of Tahiti, near the District of Vairao, on Teahaupu, the

smaller island of Tahiti (which is really two ancient inactive volcanoes with a land bridge between), ZG discovered a lovely point of land which he named Flower Point opposite one of the largest open water passages in the reef. He decided that this was where he was to establish his permanent camp. But even here, fishing was poor. He had now gone a stretch of 83 days without a single marlin strike. However, on the 84th day he captured a 464 pound striped marlin, not the Tahitian variety, but the same as those found in New Zealand and the Pacific Coast and which exceeded his own world record of 450 pounds. The significance of this long hiatus between strikes will be apparent a little later. During that trying period, ZG had become very discouraged about the fishing possibilities at Tahiti, but he was still determined to build his camp at Vairao and return there the following year to take another try for the giant marlin.

ZG had also decided that the launches he had used on this expedition, particularly those that had been carried on the deck of the *Fisherman,* were much too small and inadequate for these rough and turbulent Tahitian waters. So, he commissioned one of the finest fishing boats ever built, which he named the *Frangiapani,* after a fragrant Tahitian flower. It was built of the famous New Zealand Kauri hardwood by Collings and Bell in Auckland. But, the launch was so large that it could not be put on the deck of a freighter. Thus, Peter Williams and Frances Arledge volunteered that it would not be a great feat at all to sail this 48 foot fishing launch 2400 miles from New Zealand to Tahiti under its own power with only one stopover for fuel at Rarotonga in the Cook Islands. The voyage was completed without incident, with only the help of a sail to steady the launch and save fuel. To our knowledge, this was the first time in history that a gasoline-powered fishing launch had ever made such a long, arduous journey, but it was done without a hitch.

When ZG arrived at Vairao, the *Frangiapani* was there to greet him. This was a momentous beginning because it was here in 1930 that ZG's greatest hour as a game fisherman came. It can only be described adequately in his own words:

Suddenly I heard a sounding, vicious thump of water. Peter's feet went up in the air.

"Ge-zus!" he bawled.

His reel screeched. Quick as thought I leaned over to press my gloved hand on the whizzing spool of line. Just in time to save the reel from overrunning!

Out where Peter's bait had been showed a whirling, closing hole in the boiling white-green water. I saw a wide purple mass shooting away so close under the surface as to make the water look shallow. Peter fell out of the chair at the same instant I leaped up to straddle his rod. I had the situation in hand. My mind worked swiftly. It was an incredibly wonderful strike. The other boys piled back to the cockpit to help Peter get my other bait and the teasers in.

Before this was even started the fish ran out two hundred yards of line, then turning to the right he tore off another hundred. All in a very few seconds! Then a white splash, high as a tree, shot up, out of which leaped the most magnificent of all the leaping fish I had ever seen.

"Giant Marlin!" screamed Peter. What had happened to me I did not know, but I was cold, keen, hard, tingling, motivated to think and do the right thing. This glorious fish made a leap of thirty feet at least, low and swift, which gave me time to gauge his enormous size and his species. Here at last on the end of my line was the great Tahitian swordfish! He looked monstrous. He was pale, shiny gray in color, with broad stripes of purple. When he hit the water he sent up a splash like the flying surf on the reef.

By the time he was down I had the drag on and was winding the reel. Out he blazed again, faster, higher, longer, whirling the bonito round his head.

"Hook didn't catch!" yelled Peter, wildly. "It's on this side. He'll throw it."

I had instinctively come up mightily on the rod, winding with all speed, and I had felt the tremendous solid pull. The hook had caught before that, however, and the big bag in the line, coupled with his momentum, had set it.

"No, Peter! He's fast," I replied. Still I kept working like a windmill in a cyclone to get up the slack. The monster had circled in these two leaps. Again he burst out, a plunging leap which took him under a wall of rippling white spray. Next instant such a terrific jerk as I had never sustained nearly unseated me. He was away on his run.

"Take the wheel, Peter," I ordered, and released the drag. "Water! Somebody pour water on this reel! . . . Quick!"

The white line melted, smoked, burned off the reel. I smelled the scorching. It burned through my gloves. John was swift to plunge a bucket overboard and douse reel, rod, and me with water. That, too, saved us.

"After him, Pete!" I called, piercingly. The engines roared and the launch danced around to leap in the direction of the tight line.

"Full speed!" I yelled.

"Aye, sir," yelled Peter, who had been a sailor before he became a whaler and a fisherman. Then we had our race. It was thrilling in the extreme, and though brief it was far too long for me. Five hundred yards from us — over a third of a mile — he came up to pound and beat the water into a maelstrom.

"Slow up!" I sang out. We were bagging the line. Then I turned on the wheel-drag and began to pump and reel as never before in all my life. How precious that big spool — that big reel handle! They fairly ate up the line. We got back two hundred yards of the 500 out before he was off again. This time, quick as I was, it took all my strength to release the drag, for when a weight is pulling hard it releases with extreme difficulty. No more risk like that!

He beat us in another race, shorter, at the end of which, when he showed like a plunging elephant, he had out four hundred and fifty yards of line.

"Too much — Peter!" I panted. "We must — get him closer — Go to it!"

So we ran down upon him. I worked as before, desperately, holding on my nerve, and when I got three hundred yards back again on the reel, I was completely winded, and the hot sweat poured off my naked arms and breast.

"He's sounding . . . Get my shirt . . . Harness!"

Warily I let go with one hand and then with the other, as John and Jimmy helped me on with my shirt and then with the leather harness. With that hooked on to my reel and the great strain transferred to my shoulders, I felt that I might not be torn asunder.

"All set. Let's go," I said, grimly. But he had gone down, which gave me a chance to get back my breath. Not long, however, did he remain down. I felt and saw the line rising.

"Keep him on the starboard quarter, Peter. Run up on him now . . . Bob, your chance for pictures!"

I was quick to grasp that the swordfish kept coming to our left, and repeatedly on that run I had Peter swerve in the same direction, in order to keep the line out on the quarter. Once we were almost in danger. But I saw it. I got back all but one hundred yards of line. Close enough! He kept edging in ahead of us, and once we had to turn halfway to keep the stern toward him. But he quickly shot ahead again. He was fast, angry, heavy. How his tail pounded the leader! The short powerful strokes vibrated all over me.

"Port — port, Peter!" I yelled, and even then, so quick was the swordfish, I missed seeing two leaps directly in front of the boat as he curved ahead of us. But the uproar from Bob and the others was enough for me. As the launch sheered around, however, I saw the third of that series of leaps — and if anything could have loosed my chained emotion on the instant that unbelievably swift and savage plunge would have done so. But I was clamped. No more dreaming! No more bliss! I was there to think and act. And I did not even thrill.

By the same tactics the swordfish sped off a hundred yards of line and by the same we recovered them and drew close to see him leap again, only two hundred feet off our starboard, a little ahead, and of all the magnificent fish I have ever seen he excelled. His power to leap was beyond credence. Captain M's big fish, that broke off two years before, did not move like this one. True, he was larger. Nevertheless, this swordfish was so huge that when he came out in dazzling swift flight, my crew went simply mad. This was the first time my natives had been flabbergasted. They were as excited, as carried away, as Bob and John. Peter, however, stuck at the wheel as if he was after a wounded whale which might any instant turn upon him. I did not need to warn Peter not to let that fish hit us. If he had he would have made splinters out of that launch. Many an anxious glance did I cast toward Cappy's boat, too great for us to be alone at the mercy of that brute, if he charged us either by accident or design. But Captain could not locate us, owing to the misty atmosphere, and missed seeing this grand fish in action.

How sensitive I was to the strain on the line! A slight slackening directed all my faculties to ascertain the cause. The light on the moment was bad, and I had to peer closely to see the line. He had not slowed up, but he was curving back and to the left again — the cunning strategist!

"Port, Peter — port!" I commanded.

We sheered, but not enough. With the wheel hard over, one engine full speed ahead, the other in reverse, we wheeled like a top. But not swift enough for that Tahitian swordfish.

The line went under the bow.

"Reverse!" I called, sharply.

We pounded on the waves, slowly caught hold, slowed, started back. Then I ordered the clutches thrown out. It was a terrible moment and took all my will not to yield to sudden blank panic.

When my line ceased to pay out I felt that it had been caught on the keel. And as I was only human, I surrendered for an instant to agony. But no! That line was new, strong, the swordfish was slowing. I could yet avert catastrophe.

"Quick, Pete! Feels as if the line is caught," I cried, unhooking my harness from the reel.

Peter complied with my order. "Yes, by cripes! It's caught. Overboard, Jimmy! Jump in! Loose the line!"

The big Tahitian in a flash was out of his shirt and bending to dive.

"No! — Hold on, Jimmy!" I yelled. Only a moment before I had seen sharks milling about. "Grab him, John!"

They held Jimmy back, and a second later I plunged my rod over the side into the water, so suddenly that the weight of it and reel nearly carried me overboard.

"Hold me — or it's all — day!" I panted, and I thought that if my swordfish had fouled on keel or propellers I did not care if I did fall in.

"Let go my line, Peter," I said, making ready to extend the rod to the limit of my arms.

"I can feel him moving, sir," shouted Peter, excitedly. "By jingo! He's coming! . . . It's free! It wasn't caught!"

That was such an intense relief I could not recover my balance. They had to haul me back into the boat. I shook all over as one with the palsy, so violently that Peter had to help me get the rod in the rod-socket of the chair. An instant later came the strong electrifying pull on the line, the scream of the reel. Never such sweet music! He was away from the boat — on a tight line! The revulsion of feeling was so great that it propelled me instantaneously back into my former state of hard, cold, calculating and critical judgment, and iron determination.

"Close shave, sir," said Peter, cheerily. "It was like when a whale turns on me, after I've struck him . . . We're all clear, sir, and after him again."

The gray pall of rain bore down on us. I was hot and wet with sweat, and asked for a raincoat to keep me from being chilled. Enveloped in this, I went on with my absorbing toil. Blisters began to smart on my hands, especially one on the inside of the third finger of my right hand, certainly a queer place to raise one. But it bothered me, hampered me. Bob put on his rubber coat and, protecting his camera more than himself, sat out on the bow, waiting.

My swordfish, with short, swift runs took us

five miles further out, and then welcome to see, brought us back, all this while without leaping, though he broke water on the surface a number of times. He never sounded after that first dive. The bane of an angler is a sounding swordfish, and here in Tahitian waters, where there is no bottom, it spells catastrophe. The marlin slowed up and took to milling, a sure sign of a rattled fish. Then he rose again, and it happened to be when the rain had ceased. He made one high, frantic jump about two hundred yards ahead of us, and then threshed on the surface, sending the bloody spray high. All on board were quick to see that sign of weakening, of tragedy — blood.

Peter turned to say, cooly, "He's our meat, sir."

I did not allow any such idea to catch my consciousness. Peter's words, like those of Bob and John, and the happy jargon of the Tahitians, had no effect upon me whatever.

It rained half an hour longer, during which we repeated several phases of the fight, except slower on the part of the marlin. In all he leaped fifteen times clear of the water. I did not attempt to keep track of his threshings.

After the rain passed I had them remove the rubber coat, which hampered me, and settled to a slower fight. About this time the natives again sighted sharks coming around the boat. I did not like this. Uncanny devils! They were the worst of these marvelous fishing waters. But Peter said: "They don't know what it's all about. They'll go away."

They did go away long enough to relieve me of dread, then they trooped back, lean, yellow-backed, white-finned wolves.

"We ought to have a rifle," I said. "Sharks won't stay to be shot at, whether hit or not."

It developed that my swordfish had leaped too often and run too swiftly to make an extremely long fight. I had expected a perceptible weakening and recognized it. So did Peter, who smiled gladly. Then I taxed myself to the utmost and spared nothing. In another hour, which seemed only a few minutes, I had him whipped and coming. I could lead him. The slow strokes of his tail took no more line. Then he quit wagging.

"Clear for action, Pete. Give John the wheel . . . I see the end of the double line . . . There!"

I heaved and wound. With the end of the double line over my reel I screwed the drag up tight. The finish was in sight. Suddenly I felt tugs and jerks at my fish.

"Sharks!" I yelled, hauling away for dear life.

Everybody leaned over the gunwale. I saw a wide shining mass, greenish silver, crossed by purple bars. It moved. It weaved. But I could drag it easily.

"*Mauu! Mauu!*" shrilled the natives.

"Heave!" shouted Peter, as he peered down.

In a few more hauls I brought the swivel of the leader out of the water.

"By God! They're on him!" roared Peter, hauling on the leader. "Get the lance, boat-hook, gaffs — anything. Fight them off! . . ."

Suddenly Peter let go the leader and jerking the big gaff from Jimmy he lunged out. There was a single enormous roar of water and a sheeted splash. I saw a blue tail so wide I thought I was crazy. It threw a six foot yellow shark into the air!

"Rope him, Charley," yelled Peter. "Rest of you fight the tigers off."

I unhooked the harness and stood up to lean over the gunwale. A swordfish rolled on the surface, extending from forward of the cockpit to two yards or more beyond the end. His barred body was as large as that of an ox. And to it sharks were clinging, tearing, out on the small part near the tail. Charley looped the great tail and that was a signal for the men to get into action.

One big shark had a hold just below the anal fin. How cruel, brutish, ferocious! Peter made a powerful stab at him. The big lance head went clear through his neck. He gulped and sank. Peter stabbed another underneath, and still another. Jimmy was tearing at sharks with the long-handled gaff, and when he hooked one he was nearly hauled overboard. Charley threshed with his rope; John did valiant work with the boathook, and Bob frightened me by his daring fury as he leaned far over to hack with the cleaver.

We keep these huge cleavers on board to use in case we are attacked by octopus, which is not a far-fetched fear at all. It was possible. Bob is lean and long and powerful. Also he was angry. Whack! He slashed a shark that let go and appeared to slip up into the air.

"On the nose, Bob. Split his nose! That's the weak spot on a shark," yelled Peter.

Next shot Bob cut deep into the round stub nose of this big black shark — the only one of that color I saw — and it had the effect of dynamite. More sharks appeared under Bob, and I was scared so stiff I could not move. "Take that! . . . And that!" sang out Bob, in a kind of fierce ecstasy. "You will try to eat our swordfish! Dirty, stinking pups! . . . Aha!"

"Look out, Bob, for God's sake, look out!" I begged, frantically, after I saw a shark almost reach Bob's arm.

Peter swore at him. But there was no keeping Bob off those cannibals. Blood and water flew all over us. The smell of sharks in any case was not pleasant, and with them spouting blood, and my giant swordfish rolling in blood, the stench that arose was sickening. They appeared to come from all directions, especially from under the boat. Finally I had to get into the thick of it, and at that armed only with a gaff handle minus the gaff. I did hit one a stunning welt over the nose, making him let go. If we had all had lances like the one Peter was using so effectively we would have made short work of them. One jab from Peter either killed or disabled a shark. The crippled ones swam about belly up or lopsided, and stuck up their heads as if to get air. Of all the bloody messes I ever saw that was the worst.

"Makes me remember the war!" panted Peter, grimly.

And it was Peter who whipped the flock of ravenous sharks off. *Cluck!* went the heavy lance, and that was the end of another. My heart apparently had ceased to function. To capture that glorious fish only to see it devoured before my eyes!

"Run ahead, Johnny, out of this bloody slaughterhole, so we can see," called Peter.

John ran forward a few rods into clear water. A few sharks followed, one of them to his death. The others grew wary, and swam around

"We got 'em licked! Say, I had the wind up me," said Peter. "Who ever saw the like of that? The bloody devils."

Bob took the remaining lance from Peter, and stuck the most venturesome of the remaining sharks. It appeared then that we had the situation in hand again. My swordfish was still there, his beautiful body bitten here and there, his tail almost severed, but not irreparably lacerated. All around the boat wounded sharks were lolling with fins out, sticking ugly heads up, to gulp and dive.

There came a let down then and we exchanged the natural elation we felt. The next thing was to see what was to be done with the monster, now we had him. I vowed we could do nothing but tow him to camp. Peter made the attempt to lift him on the boat. All six of us, hauling the ropes, could not get his back half out of the water. So we tied

him fast and started campward.

Halfway in we espied Cappy's boat. He headed for us, no doubt attracted by all the flags the boys had strung up. There was a red and blue flag that I had never flown. Jimmy tied this on his bamboo pole and tied that high on the mast. Cappy bore quickly down on us and ran alongside, he and his crew vastly excited. "What is it? Lamming big broadbill?" he yelled. My fish did resemble a broadbill in his long black beak, his widespread flukes, his purple color, shading so dark now that the broad bars showed indistinctly. Besides, he lay belly up.

"No, Cappy. He's a giant Tahitian striped marlin, one of the kind we've tried so hard to catch," I replied happily.

"By gad! So he is. What a monster! . . . I'm, glad old man. My word, I'm glad! I didn't tell you, but I was discouraged. Now we're sitting on top of the world again."

We arrived at the dock about three o'clock, to find all our camp folk and a hundred natives assembled to greet us. Up and down had sped the news of the flags waving.

I went ashore and waited impatiently to see the marlin hauled out on the sand. It took a dozen men, all wading, to drag him in. And when they at last got him under the tripod, I approached, knowing I was to have a shock and prepared for it.

But at that he surprised me in several ways. His color had grown darker and the bars showed only palely. Still they were there and helped to identify him as one of the striped species. He was bigger than I had ever hoped for. And his body was long and round. This roundness appeared to be an extraordinary feature for a marlin spearfish. His bill was three feet long, not slender and razor-like, as in the ordinary marlin, or short and bludgeon-like, as in the black marlin. It was about the same size all the way from tip to where it swelled into his snout, and slightly flattened on top — a superb and remarkable weapon. The fact that the great striped spearfish Captain Mitchell lost in 1928 had a long, curved bill, like a rhinoceros, did not deter me from pronouncing this of the same species. Right there I named this species, Giant Tahitian Striped Marlin. Singularly, he had a small head, only a foot or more from where his beak broadened to his eye, which, however, was as large as that of a broadbill swordfish. There were two gill openings on each side, a feature I never observed before in any swordfish, the one toward the mouth being considerably smaller than the regular gill opening. From there his head sheered up to his hump-back, out of which stood an enormous dorsal fin. He had a straight under maxillary. The pectoral fins were large, wide, like wings, and dark in color. The fin-like appendages under and back of his lower jaw were only about six inches long and quite slender. In other spearfish these are long, and in sailfish sometimes exceed two feet and more. His body, for eight feet was as symmetrical and round as that of a good big stallion. According to my deduction it was a male fish. He carried this roundness back to his anal fin, and there further accuracy was impossible because the sharks had eaten away most of the flesh from these fins to his tail. On one side, too, they had torn out enough meat to fill a bushel basket. His tail was the most splendid of all the fish tails I have ever observed. It was a perfect bent bow, slender, curved, dark purple in color, finely ribbed, and expressive of the tremendous speed and strength the fish had exhibited.

This tail had a spread of five feet two inches. His length was fourteen feet two inches. His girth was six feet nine inches. And his weight as he was 1,040 pounds.

Every drop of blood had been drained from his body, and this with at least 200 pounds of flesh the sharks took would have fetched his true and natural weight to 1,250 pounds. But I thought it best to have the record stand at the actual weight, without allowing for what he had lost. Nevertheless, despite my satisfaction and elation, as I looked up at his appalling shape, I could not help but remember the giant marlin Mitchell had lost in 1928, which we estimated at twenty-two or twenty-three feet, or the twenty-foot one I had raised at Tautira, or the twenty-eight foot one the natives had seen repeatedly alongside their canoes. And I thought of the prodigious leaps and astounding fleetness of this one I had caught. "MY heaven!" I breathed. "What would a bigger one do?"

This was truly ZG's greatest triumph. He had finally succeeded in beating Mitchell's record and had broken the world record for all-tackle gamefish. But the record that should have been his was denied him. At that time, the American Museum of Natural History, which had commenced to keep the big game fishing world records at the time, refused to accept this record as valid, even though the affidavits of all those on board the *Frangiapani* stated that the sharks had not touched the giant marlin until after he had been gaffed. Mutilation of a fish prior to landing was considered a disqualification. However, though ZG called it a Giant Tahitian Striped Marlin, it was actually a Pacific Blue Marlin, which is the name by which this species is known. Many had been landed near Hawaii but none of such size. Contrasted with a Striped Marlin, the Blue generally has different dimensions: the eye closer to the bill of the fish; somewhat rounder, more symmetrical than the striped cousin; and a much greater size. From ZG's dimensions measured of this great catch, it probably would have weighed in the neighborhood of 1200 to 1300 pounds had it not been mutilated by the sharks, and would probably have been a world record up until the time a 1300 pound Blue was landed off Kona, Hawaii, in 1983. With all the meat eaten away and the blood loss, it still weighed 1040 pounds and for more than twenty-five years no other fisherman came close to landing any game fish as large until Albert Glassell brought to gaff his giant black marlin off Cabo Blanco, Peru, in 1956. It weighed 1560 pounds and is still the all-tackle record for gamefish, other than sharks, today.

ZG was to visit Tahiti three more times, in 1931, 1934, and 1938, and was to land a number of large fish, including a bright silver-colored fish that resembled a Black but which he named a Silver Marlin. For a time it was scientifically considered a new species, until some bureaucrat in Washington, in his infinite wisdom, decided to call it an Albino Black. As a result the only record which had been accepted by the newly founded IGFA was also denied him. He raised several more of the giant Blues during this time, but none were ever landed.

The Fisherman I *at anchor near Apataki,*
Tuamotu Islands, on the 1929 expedition.

*This scenic view of Tahiti shows Zane Grey's
camp at "Flower Point," Vairao, Tahiti.*

ZG found that he needed extra heavy duty gear to tackle the monsters of the South Pacific and had this reel, the largest ever made, built for him by Arthur Kovalovsky. Today the reel is in the Zane Grey Museum at Zanesville, Ohio. The author's pride in his invention is indicated by his signature on this photo.

*Even after hours of battle, ZG's record
1,040-pound marlin continued to
struggle until the end. After the giant
creature was hauled in and weighed,
the chief of the district of Vairao,
Tahiti came out with his entourage to
congratulate the intrepid fisherman.*

Though it could pass for a tranquil brook along the Thames, this photograph actually captures ZG as he attempts to land one of the famed nato *trout, native to Vairao, Tahiti.*

By day's end, ZG had captured at least a specimen of the nato, *the South Pacific's nearest equivalent to the North American trout.*

*Zane Grey with secretary, Wanda Williams,
Dr. and Mrs. Wiborn, and Chief Mauu of the
district of Papieri, Tahiti. In Tahitian, Mauu
means "shark." That was probably the right
name for the chief since he sold ZG the land
around his dock for a "good price"; but it
turned out it was not his to sell.*

This photo, taken by Loren, seems to evoke the awesome grandeur of the South Pacific, showing the yacht Frangiapani *standing off the dock at Vairao, Tahiti in a glorious sunset.*

The Voyage of Fisherman II

After the disappointment of being denied his record, ZG vowed to go on to greater undiscovered fishing grounds. He decided that *Fisherman I* was too slow and, in his eyes, inadequate for the voyage of his dreams. His determination was to take him clear into the Indian Ocean where he had heard tales of giant sailfish up to twenty-five feet long just waiting to be captured. So, *Fisherman I* was sold to Father Rougier, a French priest, who purchased it to haul copra from his various island properties to Tahiti.

ZG soon found the potential new yacht of his dreams, a sailing vessel called the *Kallisto,* which had been made by Krupps in Germany. She was a beautiful, slim sailing yacht and had once broken a speed record for crossing the Atlantic Ocean. She was 186 feet long but only 28 feet in beam, compared to the 38 foot beam of *Fisherman I.* ZG spent over $300,000 in removing the masts and sails, putting in more powerful engines and outfitting the ship with no less than six fishing launches — two of which were 34 feet long. Unfortunately, the *Fisherman II,* as he renamed it, proved to be a Jonah. Not only was she much more expensive to operate than the *Fisherman I* had been, but she was unseaworthy as well. On her first bout with a storm outside Moorea, the vessel nearly foundered, but ZG was still determined to continue on the voyage. *Fisherman II* sailed first to Raiatea, Bora Bora, then the Tonga Islands — where ZG did break his own sailfish world record with a catch of 170 pounds — and finally on to Fiji. However, this was where the great new Odyssey came to an abrupt and dismal end. ZG received a fateful telegram from Dolly saying that there was no more money left to continue on, and only barely enough to return home. His dream of the grandiose voyage through the Straights of Carpinteria into the Indian Ocean and the mysterious Cocos and Mauritius Islands and their twenty-five foot sailfish, was never to take place. The ship returned to Los Angeles, sat ignominiously at the Todd shipyard in San Pedro for nearly four years and was finally sold for $10,000 to be used as a tuna boat.

But ZG was undaunted. Just over a year later he approached the Vanderbilts with the idea of conducting a joint scientific fishing voyage with them, making a film from this, and sharing the profits. They appeared interested but finally turned his offer down. So, in desperation, he turned to Ernest Hemingway. His relationship with Hemingway, who had only recently become famous, was something of an armed neutrality. My feeling is that ZG was jealous of Hemingway's writing prowess and at the same time Hemingway was even more jealous of my father's fishing prowess and, of course, his supposed immense wealth (which was by this time nearly all dissipated). ZG's offer to Hemingway was similar in nature to the one he had made to the Vanderbilts. However, according to Carlos Baker, one of Hemingway's biographers, Hemingway turned the offer down and told all of his friends that ZG was trading on *his* fishing reputation, which even Baker admitted was somewhat absurd, considering that ZG had already amassed nine world deep sea fishing records and Hemingway had none.

However, in an effort to interest him in the possibility of the joint venture, ZG had sent Hemingway a copy of *Tales of Tahitian Waters,* in which the story of his capture of his giant marlin was told. This had, at least, a rather amazing result. In my first reading of *The Old Man and the Sea,* Hemingway's Nobel Prize winning novel which first was published in *Life* magazine in 1940, I realized that there had been kinship between the two men, which both had somehow recognized but never expressed. ZG had gone 83 days without a strike during his long 1929-30 trips to Tahiti. On the 84th day he broke his own world record for striped marlin. Then only a few weeks later he landed his giant blue marlin, only to have it disqualified because of the huge amounts of flesh the sharks had eaten away on one side. In *The Old Man and the Sea,* Hemingway's native hero goes out from Florida in his little boat over and over again and endures 83 days without a single strike. On the 84th day he hooks his giant marlin which tows him for days, finally leaps itself into a frenzy and he captures it. (Incidentally, in the movie, the giant marlin leaping was Albert Glassell's 1560 pound black. They do have stripes when they are alive, but which fade when they die). After he lashes his great quarry to his boat and commences his journey home, the sharks come. By the time he reaches port the sharks have eaten the entire fish down to only a huge skeleton. Whether Hemingway had consciously used this part of ZG's account will never be known. But, Hemingway, in his masterful fashion somehow had summed up, as eloquently as has ever been done, much of what ZG had written about during all his years, both as a novelist and fisherman: the unending struggle of man against the elements and nature and against the wild creatures who fight against it and one another to survive.

Tetiaroa

In spite of the disasters of the *Fisherman II,* the full onset of the great Depression of the 1930s, and his failure to secure a partner for his hoped-for new ventures, ZG was still able to continue his travels, albeit at a much reduced scale, largely because of Dolly's business acumen. Even during the days of his greatest wealth, he always gave half of his earnings to Dolly. Her investments managed to provide enough money for trips to Oregon in 1932 and another voyage to Tahiti in 1934. It was during this year that my fishing partner, Johnny Vitalich, and I accompanied him and we spent three extraordinary weeks on a tiny, then almost unknown atoll named Tetiaroa. It now has another claim to fame — if one can call it that — in the fact that it is now owned by actor Marlon Brando. Tetiaroa is almost entirely unnoticed by tourists — or anyone who visits Tahiti, for that matter — except occasionally when it can be seen from the great jet planes from Hawaii which sweep down over it toward a landing at Tahiti's Faaa airfield just a few miles west of Papeete. The island is only about ten miles long and perhaps five miles wide at its widest point, and is located about thirty-five miles northwest of Tahiti. There is no passage in the reef, so landings must be made either over the reef or by plane. At the time we visited it in 1934, the island was owned by Dr. Williams, a retired British dentist, who, when contacted, agreed to let us spend time there to do some exploring. There is one point on the lee side of the island away from the trade winds where the reef, instead of curving down so that the waves curl over and smash against it with too much force to risk a landing, extends straight out and then drops off

abruptly. As a result, except in very heavy weather, waves rise up and flow over the reef and then drop down back off the reef in a smooth progression. On the very point of this part of the reef, the owner had built a small dock on concrete pilings attached to the coral of the reef. A brief anchorage about thirty to fifty feet deep extends off the reef about one hundred feet off shore. As long as the trade winds blow from the southeast, small vessels could anchor here and stay safely off the reef.

However, when it came to loading the considerable amount of baggage and camping equipment that was necessary to take ashore, we found that the dock was totally inadequate. Another factor that made it difficult was that there was no walkway from the dock to the shore. One had to climb down from the dock into a shallow, fringing reef and wade to shore in water about five feet deep, a matter of about a quarter-mile. The only other way to land was to row a boat up to the edge of the reef, wait until the waves were washing over and then to row very quickly — the water would then subside and the boat would be sitting on the reef until the next advancing wave would then push it in further. By this very laborious and sometimes hazardous process, we dragged all our tents and camping equipment ashore and made camp on the main island. Here, the protected land was away from the trade winds and was as high as any part of the atoll — probably fifteen feet above sea level. Here, a small forest of giant, gnarled trees — the names of which I do not know — grew and provided what shade there was on the island. The dentist had built his stone house and lived alone, except for native servants, among these trees. It was well screened and fairly comfortable. However, we were required to live in tents, although Williams did condescend to invite us to dinner one evening at his home.

The living conditions here were, to say the least, appalling. There were simply clouds of mosquitos; during mealtime the only way to protect oneself from them was to sit in the smoke of the camp fire — that or be eaten alive. At least our tents were screened and at night we would spray the entire inside of the tents to kill the mosquitos so we could sleep. Outside, because this was February and the middle of summer, the beach, not being sand but rough bits of coral, was so blindingly white and hot that one could not look down at it at midday without sunglasses. But in the shallow and deeper water above the reef, near the shore, was the most astounding sight I have ever seen. The temperature of the water here was probably 90 degrees and we could see literally millions of fish of all sizes, shapes, and descriptions darting to and fro.

The large fish, such as crevalle and huge Spanish mackerel, were slashing into the smaller ones from deeper water. The reefs near Tahiti and the other islands, though colorful, were extremely barren compared to this. As well, there were sharks everywhere. However, in the shallow water they were very small, some of them only two to three feet in length. They did not bother us in this shallow water, although none of us dared to swim out any farther than to where the depth of the water was over four or five feet. Also, in the interior of the island, behind our host's cabin, was a large grove of coconut trees. One of the weirdest sights imaginable was to be seen at night when walking outdoors with a flashlight and coming upon dozens of pairs of eyes as big as humans' shining back at us. The foot of each tree was inhabited by huge coconut land crabs, some of them as large as three feet across, which stayed underground during the day but came out at night. For the most part they subsisted on the remnants of the coconuts that had fallen on the ground and dried up. They ate what was left of the interior after tearing them apart with their huge claws.

ZG had noticed another point of interest while he was walking along the north end of the main island facing the lagoon. In front of the fringe of islets that ran across the northern flank of Tetiaroa was what looked like a coral flat — one that appeared to be similar to those on which he had fished in Florida. ZG came back very excited that day and said, "I'll bet there are bonefish on that flat." So, the next day we piled in our boats and rowed across the lagoon, a matter of about two miles. Unfortunately, we did not think to bring outboard motors on the boats, which hindered our exploration of the island. We did find such a coral flat — one that in Florida terms was very small — about a mile long and half a mile wide. But it had the requisites and we did discover bonefish there.

I had never fished for bonefish before. My first experience of bait-casting for these elusive fish was to throw my entire rod and reel thirty feet away from the boat into the water. I sneaked down into the shallow flat and retrieved the rod, hoping that ZG in the other boat nearby had not seen me, but I was unfortunately wrong and he had great glee in telling the whole camp about it that evening. That morning, Johnny and I hooked a couple of bonefish, both of which promptly ran down off the narrow flat into the deeper water and cut the line on the coral. I also saw two or three much larger, bluer looking fish which I could not identify.

Dad, being more of an expert, had fared better. In his boat was Brownella Baker, his secretary, and each had caught a bonefish — possibly the first bonefish ever landed on rod and reel in the South Pacific. He also swore that the large blue fish we had seen were also bonefish. In fact, he called them black bonefish and stated he had hooked at least two and they had run off all his line or had broken it in the coral heads in the deeper water. He estimated that the largest ones could weigh as heavy as 25 pounds. (As mentioned before, the world record for bonefish is still only a little over 16 pounds.)

However, the most intriguing aspect of our Tetiaroa trip took place during the few days we went fishing on one of the launches outside the island, before the weather turned bad. The first day, Johnny and I went out alone on the *Frangiapani* with a native guide and our regular boatman, who was part Tahitian and part French and could speak some English. The conversations with the native indicated that they were both aware of the underbilled swordfish that had been described to ZG by the natives in Rangiroa several years before. The guide and boatman told us that there were two species known. One was like a tropical fish commonly found in the Atlantic waters, called a Ballyhoo, which resembled a tiny broadbill but with the bill on the lower jaw. However, in the Atlantic this fish grows to a length of only about twenty inches; but here the natives stated they could be as large as 10 feet long. The other fish they mentioned was one that appeared more like a marlin and sometimes grew very large. Both of them were apparently only to be found in very deep water. However, as we were trolling along the North shore of Tetiaroa about a mile from the reef on that first day, one of the strangest looking creatures that I have ever seen came up behind our bait. He was very dark, almost jet black, with a faint reddish tinge, and looked to be about ten to twelve feet long. He looked totally unlike anything I had ever seen before and followed the bait for some distance. John, who was on top of the cabin, said that when he turned sideways he was sure this was one of the famed swordfish with a bill on the under jaw. Later, we were told by natives who lived on the island that if we had stopped the boat and let the bait back we might have had a chance to have gotten a strike from this fish.

Two days later when I was fishing with ZG — one of the few times I was ever on the same boat with him — I had a rousing strike from a marlin that made some magnificent jumps before he broke the leader. I was not sure it was anything more than a dark blue striped marlin. Of course, ZG's comments on it were considerably different:

It happened right then and there. I was always ready, always alert, having been taught that by innumerable surprises and disasters. It was I who saw the blue flash and pealed out the warning yell. But the fish had Loren's bait and was gone before you could wink. I saw only his broad-lobed deep-blue tail — a new color and shape for me.

The line whistled off Loren's reel. Peter threw out the clutch. Rearea and Charley hauled at the teasers, yelling in their Tahitian tongue. Then the fish broke water, but did not show distinctly. Still we all saw it was a spearfish. Loren set the drag and jerked. He hooked the fish solidly. We all whooped at that.

The tight line curved back toward the wake of the boat. Then, less than one hundred and fifty feet from us, the spearfish leaped broadside, with his head pointed slightly toward us.

"Miti! Miti!" yelled Mapui. This was the first time I had heard the native name for the underbilled swordfish. I was incapable of yelling. A bursting hot gush of blood, a paralyzing joy, inhibited all my faculties except sight and thought. The spearfish was an underbill. I had never seen any fish like him. He was a beautiful dark blue without stripes. His dorsal stood up like a mane. It appeared close to his shoulders, like the fin on a black marlin. His body was deep for so small a fish. His weight could not have exceeded two hundred pounds. His head slanted markedly toward the slender rapier-like spear — the finest, most delicate spear I had ever seen. It slanted to a snub nose that resembled the marlin I had caught with bills broken off close. And under this snub nose, and out from it stuck the bill.

All in a flash I saw this. It was photographed on my brain. The underbill spearfish went down, but I had identified him absolutely. No psychology could ever dissuade me otherwise. As I had never before seen a spearfish of that species I had no preconceived picture of one in my consciousness. I could scarcely have imagined the details I saw. The moment for me was devastatingly tragic with disappointment that I had not hooked the rare fish I had made known to the world. Hard on that flooded my joy for Loren. The unclassified fish would bear his name.

There was tense excitement on board. I could never recall what was said and done. Of course all had identified the underbill.

"Aw!" cried Loren, in piercing anguish.

His line had gone slack. The fish had gotten off. As I had never experienced such a profound exultance so now I experienced a shock of grief that froze me cold and sick. Peter stuttered in his outburst of bitter regret. The natives stood silent.

Loren appeared afraid to reel in the line. His head sank over the reel. I divined that his emotion was due to the fear that he had had a chance to catch the rarest, the most wonderful fish in the sea, and he had failed. His grief overcame my own.

"Reel in, son. Let's see — what —," I said, huskily. The twelve thread leader had been severed in the middle. The end came in coiled like a corkscrew. It had been wrapped around the spear of the fish, and had either been cut or unequal to the strain.

Loren stared at it — at the stiff coil that would not straighten out. Then he looked up at me with eyes hard to meet.

"Dad!" he besought me, poignantly.

So, if he was right in his observation, I may have had the distinction of having hooked and lost the first swordfish of this species on record. At least I still like to think this might be what happened. After my sighting of the great shark, I am inclined to believe that his description probably was more accurate than I had thought at the time. Perhaps some day I will go back to Tetiaroa and find that elusive underbilled marlin or at least the enormous shark that may still be living somewhere in the mysterious Tuamotu Islands.

ZG's Writing about Tahiti

Another achievement that ZG made during his visits to Tahiti must also be noted here. As had so many famous writers before him, he had always been fascinated by the curious melange of racial characteristics of the inhabitants of Tahiti and other Polynesian Islands and their casual attitudes about sex and life, and also their marvelous love of children regardless of race or color. During one of the trips I remember meeting a couple who lived down the road just around the corner from our camp at Vairao. The father and mother were Tahitians; the children included three from the father, and of the other three, one was half-white, one was half-Oriental, and one was half-Indian. Even at that time in the 1930s, the women were still fascinated by the white men and it was considered an honor for a Tahitian woman to bear a child by a white man. Of course, the native men were not as eager about this as were the women, but at that time life was so easy in Tahiti that no one seemed to care about those relationships — one had merely to spear a few fish or pull a breadfruit down from a tree for an ample meal. The government provided enough work so that the men could work to earn the few francs needed to buy sugar, salt, the few commodities that would be purchased from the itinerant Chinese stores which were everywhere on the island. We saw also, some of the ways in which the French authorities treated the natives in Tahiti. It was not in the least persecution, but rather something of benevolent neglect.

This was something not necessarily true of other places such as the Island of Makatea, where the French imported Vietnamese to work the guano fields. Makatea is an upraised coral atoll about 125 miles northeast of Tahiti and at that time the dried up lagoon was filled with centuries upon centuries of bird droppings as well as carcasses of millions of fish which furnished some of the richest fertilizer in the world. Most of the Tahitians on the local islands refused to work in these fields so the French imported Annamites, as they were called, from Vietnam and Cambodia, to work the fields. Once these workers reached the island, the only place they were able to buy food or supplies was at the local store and the French set the prices so high that none of them ever got out of debt. They lived in virtual slavery. The work, which consisted of hand-digging the guano by shovels out of the countless coral pockets that covered the island, was back-breaking in the tropic heat. Workers were paid one franc per ton (about three cents at the rate of exchange at the time of visiting Makatea). A hard worker could dig perhaps ten tons a day. When the jagged coral pockets deepened, ladders were put down and the guano was hauled up in large containers. I visited Makatea in 1938 and was determined to write a novel exposing the inhumane conditions which existed there. But the War intervened, and after Vietnam, the French found fewer and fewer workers to dig. I learned only a year or two ago that the guano in the pits had finally been exhausted and the French had departed. The island is perhaps now uninhabited, except for a small band of natives who live in a tiny fringe of land on the lush southeast shore of the island facing the trade winds. This can only be reached from the top of the island through a tunnel in the ancient reef on steps that I was told had been hand-carved by a race long since vanished from Makatea. Another mystery that anthropologists may some day try to solve!

The result of my father's visits in Tahiti and his fascination with the culture resulted finally in what was probably his most exotic novel, *The Reef Girl*. The theme is the story of a beautiful, half-caste girl who had been educated by her English father in New Zealand, who hated white men and "drove them to their ruin," as ZG expressed it. Faaone's favorite pastime was to swim naked through the waves that thundered on Tahiti's reefs. She finally meets an idealistic American writer, they fall in love and live together without benefit of marriage at Tautiroa on Tahiti's north coast. Of course, this novel was totally different from anything he had previously written. For years publishers would have nothing to do with it. Finally, after some judicious editing, not necessarily to change the explicitness of the sexual situations but to modernize it in keeping with today's fiction, I submitted it to Harper & Row in the spring of 1977. To my considerable surprise, they published it with some enthusiasm but unfortunately never followed it up with any promotional campaign. After the hardcover printing was sold, it was then sent to Ace Paperbacks, where the sales were not up to what is usually expected of Zane Grey novels. However, it is one of the most fascinating, as well as historically accurate accounts of modern Tahiti ever written, and there is no question in my mind that some day the right producer will see its value and make it a top notch movie.

Australia: The Final Challenge

When the Australian government found out what had happened to tourism in New Zealand after ZG's visit, they were eager to have him come to Australia. He was also anxious to find out about Australia because it was as much a virgin territory for angling as New Zealand had been in the 1920s — or even more so because there were fewer, if any, deep sea fishermen there. In January of 1936 ZG embarked on the *SS Monterey* for Australia. As with his early fishing in New Zealand, his excursion to Australia was an outstanding success. He caught numerous marlin, including a 460-pound black which set an Australian record, landed the first yellowfin tuna known there, and captured a monstrous world-record 1031 pound tiger shark just two miles off the entrance to Sydney Harbor, with the ships sailing to and fro as he was fighting the fish. He caught many varieties of sharks and learned for the first time the problems Australians experienced with man-eating sharks. More people had been bitten and injured by sharks there than anywhere else in the world. American scientists naively believed at that time that sharks would not attack a white man. ZG was so incensed by this that when he returned from Australia he vowed to write a book strictly about shark attacks on humans. We still have the file of over a hundred such incidents, mostly occurring on the beaches of Australia. It was not until World War II when a U.S. anti-aircraft cruiser, the Juneau, was sunk by a Japanese submarine not far from Guadalcanal and almost half the survivors were eaten by sharks, that the American military and the scientists woke up to the fact that sharks could be extremely dangerous under any circumstances.

One of the most ambitious undertakings that ZG ever conceived of was to film his own movie about the great white pointer shark which he had named White Death, the name by which it is known today. He journeyed nearly a thousand miles north of Sydney, where on Haymen Island, which now houses one of the finest resorts on the Australian coast inside the Great Barrier Reef, he filmed the only full-length movie he ever produced and starred in himself. The plot was simple: a white shark was terrorizing the inhabitants of a village and ZG catches the shark. I would guess that Peter Benchley, the author of *Jaws*, probably had not been born or at least was not doing much writing at that time. Unfortunately, the movie was so poorly made that it was a financial failure but it is certainly worth viewing as a curiosity and an example of the kind of pioneer filmmaking ZG indulged in.

Fisherman II

*ZG (third from left) undertaking the perilous journey
by skiff over the barrier reef at Tetiaroa.*

*The land crabs on Tetiaroa were enormous.
ZG and other members of the party enjoyed
taking a brief time out to observe their
exotic behavior.*

ZG with a pair of bonefish caught near Tetiaroa — an island today best known as Marlon Brando's South Pacific home. There is reason to believe that this catch, in 1934, may be the first recorded catch of bonefish in the South Pacific.

The writer's 1,036-pound tiger shark, caught off Sydney Head, Australia was a world record in 1936. ZG felt that catches like this one would help to prove the size and strength of sharks and to prove that these sea monsters were, indeed, dangerous to humans.

At his writing desk, ZG examines the jawbone and tooth structure of his 1,036-pound world-record tiger shark.

*ZG with rare fox thresher shark caught off
the coast of Australia in 1937.*

*Signed photo of Zane Grey with his catch of
six grey nurse sharks caught off Bermagui,
Australia in 1936.*

(Left) *ZG with 460-pound Australian record
black marlin caught off Bermagui in 1936.*
(Above) *Inspecting the razor-sharp teeth of
the 800-pound "death shark" caught off the
Australian coast.*

The writer appears in a still photograph from the movie, White Death, *fighting the great white shark. The film was a precursor of Peter Benchley's* Jaws. *(Right) With Nola Warren, star of the ZG-produced movie,* White Death.

The End
of the Trail

After ZG had left the Rogue River for good, his friend, Fred Burnham, the famous fly angler, told him of the marvelous summer steelhead which traveled up the North Umpqua River which runs by Roseburg about a hundred miles north of the Rogue. ZG's first visit there was in 1932. I had been skippering a swordfish charter boat at Catalina during my summers away from college, but ZG became so excited about this fishing that he finally convinced me to spend a summer there with him. I first visited the North Umpqua in 1935. It was a totally different experience from fishing on the Rogue. The steelhead were larger, faster, and instead of bouncing the fly across the bottom in slow water, one carefully worked it across the stream on the surface in much swifter and shallower runs. The steelhead would come at a great rush to the surface to take the fly. The fighting qualities of Rogue steelhead were probably just as great but the Umpqua's fish were much larger, averaging six to eight pounds apiece. Some went as high as twelve to fifteen pounds, and the smallest was usually at least twenty inches long. I served my apprenticeship in 1935, caught my first steelhead and landed eight fish that year.

1936 was the great summer. The river became very low and a huge run of fish came in near our camp and stopped going up river when the water warmed. In those days, ninety percent of the steelhead traveled up Steamboat Creek, the main tributary entering the river here, to spawn in the fall and spring. Usually Steamboat Creek became too hot for the steelhead to endure in the summer, so they lingered in the river until the fall rains cooled the water, then they would go up Steamboat Creek. We had established a camp at Williams Creek, across the river about a mile below Steamboat. During that incredible summer, I caught over a hundred steelhead, including one of twelve and one-half pounds, in less than two months of fishing. ZG caught sixty-five or more, many with weights up to ten or eleven pounds. Romer, who

fished only during our last 3 weeks there, landed a fish on our last day before breaking camp that was larger than any of the others, but because he didn't want to spoil my record, he never told me how much it weighed. As it happened, all three of us, Romer, ZG, and I wrote and published stories about this experience in different sporting magazines at different times. For me it was one of the greatest fishing summers I have ever encountered. It also brought me back to the North Umpqua in 1948 and for nearly every summer thereafter, until 1983.

The next year was when it all came to an end. We had come to the Umpqua during the middle of July. The fishing was poor because the river was very high and cold. On one very hot day, ZG fell asleep in the sun when the temperature was over 100 degrees in the shade. He suffered a severe sunstroke, which paralyzed his right side and inhibited his speech. This, in effect, ended his fishing, or at least so we thought. After we returned to Altadena, he refused to go to the hospital but recuperated at home, accepting only the services of our faithful old family physician, Dr. Greengo.

ZG made one more trip to Tahiti in 1937, but was still unable to fish. His final voyage was to Australia, where he caught an 800 pound white death shark early in February of 1939. That final battle probably weakened his heart and hastened the inevitable.

It was a tragic two years. He could write very little because he could not use his right hand, but he practiced signing his name over 12,000 times — I recently found the sheet where he had listed this total over the two year period. The two novels he did complete were dictated, and not of the same quality as the others. It appears likely that his exertions in his victory over the Australian shark weakened him so much that when he returned home that spring he was exhausted. On the morning of October 23, 1939, he suffered a massive rupture of the right ventricle of his heart and died instantly.

The author's study, around 1937, contained relics of his great fishing adventures around the world.

There was an air of peace when he returned in search of steelhead trout on the North Umpqua River, Oregon, in 1936. This handsome brace provided a fine meal for the author and his party.

As an acknowledgement of his international renown, the launching of the Liberty Ship Zane Grey in 1943 paid tribute to the reputation and importance of the writer who best portrayed the heritage of the West.

Loren's 11-pound steelhead caught on the North Umpqua River, around 1955, was a sample of the treasures ZG and his crew had gone after on the famed Northwestern river.

THE LAST TRAIL

After the writer's death in 1939, the cartoonist, Shoemaker, portrayed the Spirit of Zane Grey joining his most famous character in cowboy heaven.

In a sense, it was probably fitting that he passed away when he did. The War was already closing down on the world and he would not have been able to travel as before. Even if he had recovered enough to write, he would not have been able to fish in any of his old haunts. That would have killed him if nothing else. But he was by no means forgotten. Three years after his death he was accorded a special kind of recognition by having a Liberty ship named the *Zane Grey,* launched at the Terminal Island Shipyard in January of 1943. I was fortunate enough to be on leave from my Navy duties to witness that launching, and it was attended by a number of Hollywood luminaries in addition to family and friends.

The pictorial record of his exploits as shown here, perhaps does not do justice to all he accomplished, but it is a record of what he saw and did. He lived life as he believed it and wrote as he felt. Probably no one has written more compellingly about the out-of-doors or as well about conservation and the need to save our wilderness areas even at that early time. He argued long and passionately about the urgency of preserving these resources, not only for pleasure but for commercial use as well. In these photographs, we can see a different view of the man than we were able to see in his writings. Also, perhaps this book will help to add more vivid and impressive documentation to one of the most extraordinary careers that has ever been celebrated, whether in words or pictures.